JB JOSSEY-BASS™
A Wiley Brand

Turning to Business for Support

How to Increase Gift Support From Businesses and Corporations

Scott C. Stevenson, Editor

WILEY

978-1-118-69218-9   ISBN

978-1-118-70400-4   ISBN (online)

Turning to Business for Support
How to Increase Gift Support
From Businesses and Corporations

Published by

Stevenson, Inc.

P.O. Box 4528 • Sioux City, Iowa • 51104

Phone 712.239.3010 • Fax 712.239.2166

www.stevensoninc.com

TABLE OF CONTENTS

TABLE OF CONTENTS

- *10 Solicitation Mistakes to Avoid*
- *Don't Interpret 'No' as 'Never'*
- *Perfect the Art of Solicitation Small Talk*
- *Balance Solicitation Team*
- *How to Respond When Business and Philanthropy Get Mixed*
- *Dealing With Donors Who Get the Jump On You*
- *Savvy Solicitation*
- *Encourage Businesses to Give Percentage of Profits*

Chapter 6: **Provide Benefits Tailored to Businesses** 27
- *Identify Perks for Business Donors*
- *Play Up Your Most Appealing Donor Perks*
- *What About a Special Club for Business Contributors?*
- *Solicitation Strategies: Ask Funders to Become Partners*
- *When Asking Funders to Be Partners, Know It Isn't About You*
- *Match Partners With Appropriate Programs*
- *Match Corporate Needs to Sponsorship Level Benefits*
- *The Five Benefits of Corporate Sponsorships*
- *Garner Business Support With WIIFM Approach*
- *Give Business Contributors Special Status*
- *Be the Best at Honoring Event Sponsors*
- *Recognize What's In It for the Corporate Donor*

Chapter 7: **Offer Sponsorship as One Viable Option** 31
- *Personal Connections Help Secure Sponsorships*
- *Sponsorship Tips*
- *Proposals Play a Key Role in Landing Sponsorships*
- *Have You Considered a Sponsorship Menu*
- *Secure Sponsorships by Packaging All Special Events*
- *Advice for Securing Sponsorships*
- *Corporate Sponsorship Commitment Form Helps Track Sponsorships*
- *Find Companies to Sponsor Your Website*
- *Get Businesses, Corporations to Sponsor Your Volunteers*
- *Advance Businesses From Sponsors to Major Donors*

Chapter 8: **Great Ideas for Raising Gifts From Businesses** 37
- *Encourage Businesses to Set Up a Matching Gift Program*
- *Don't Overlook Generational Businesses*
- *How to Chalk Up $25,000 in New Gifts From Businesses*
- *Employees Help Children by Staying Home*
- *Involve Architects, Engineers, Contractors*
- *Four Ways to Increase Local Business Support*
- *Business Advisory Council Generates $50,000*
- *Identify Businesses That Match Hours Instead of Dollars*
- *Corporate Gift Idea*
- *Donors Invited to Give Square Feet*
- *Consultant Boosts College's Annual Campaign*

Chapter 9: **Ways to Recognize and Steward Business Donors** 42
- *Key Stewardship Relations Practices*
- *Donation Stewardship Outlined in Policy*
- *The Obligations of Stewardship, University of Notre Dame (Notre Dame, IN):*
- *Program Helps Attract Business Support and Recognize Past Donors*
- *Promote Businesses That Support Your Work*
- *Don't Underestimate the Power of a Donor Wall*
- *Show Donors the Money (and Where it Goes)*
- *Website Offers Giving Tools*
- *Work With PR Staff to Publicize Key Gifts*
- *Acknowledge Matching Gifts With a Postcard*
- *Encourage Employees to Thank Their Employers*
- *Unique Illustration Recognizes Top Donors*

Turning to Business for Support: How to Increase Gift Support from Businesses & Corporations

GETTING A BUSINESS SOLICITATION EFFORT UP AND RUNNING

To get more businesses and corporations supporting your organization, it's important to convey what's in it for them. And to begin that process, we turn to the three i's: interest leads to involvement and involvement results in investment. Examine the ways in which you currently capture businesses' interest. What more can you do to set your organization apart from other worthy charities? How can you better align your organization with particular businesses?

Work to Increase Annual Support From Your Community's Businesses

Are you getting your fair share of annual gifts from the business community?

To increase support from businesses, explore what more your nonprofit can do (based on your mission) to cater to business interests.

Here are generic ideas to consider:

- Offer training of some sort for businesses' employees.
- Bring your nonprofits' services directly to businesses.
- Do your part to influence local economic development.

- Offer weekly or monthly programs at your facility covering topics of interest to businesses.
- Take on a community service project that will be noticed and appreciated by businesses.
- Offer events geared to businesses (e.g., cultural, recreational, leisure) that address quality of life.
- Address local problems (e.g., crime, health) that negatively impact the business climate.
- Become a resource center for businesses.

Create a Handout Geared to Area Businesses

When calling on businesses in your community and service area, it's important to have a marketing piece that speaks directly to them and their organization. Printed information that could easily be tailored to business contacts includes:

- ✓ A list of all businesses that contributed during the past fiscal year (possibly arranged by giving clubs or levels).
- ✓ Messages that speak to your organization's impact on the local economy (i.e., number of employees, payroll, contributions, etc.).
- ✓ Brief testimonials from respected business leaders (both large and small businesses).

- ✓ Perks (for businesses) for giving at various levels.
- ✓ Profiles of partnerships between your organization and businesses.
- ✓ Messages about how your organization positively impacts the quality of life in your community.
- ✓ A separate list of businesses sponsoring various programs throughout the past year.
- ✓ Examples of how your organization participates as a corporate citizen (i.e., chamber member, representation on boards, etc.).

Plan a Tour of Corporate Offices Event

To broaden your base of donor support, identify new ways of connecting with and involving businesses and corporate decision makers.

Want to connect with corporate decision makers and raise funds at the same time? Organize a tour of corporate offices in your community.

Base the event on the traditional tour of homes event, applying the same planning procedures for a tour of corporate facilities, especially CEO offices, that the average person rarely sees. Here's how:

1. Identify those corporations and CEO offices you prefer to include on your tour. Prioritize your top choices based on drawing card appeal and decision makers with whom you would most like to build a relationship.

2. Contact the identified CEOs (or other top decision

makers) to invite their participation, illustrate benefits and lock in the date of your event. Explain that paying guests will make stops at each corporate tour location to spend about 20 minutes touring lobbies, CEO offices and other points of interest.

3. Involve each corporate participant in planning. Involve each corporate contact in identifying anyone they want to include on the list. Discuss where to focus tour time when each bus load of guests arrives. Iron out details such as decorations, tour procedures, giveaways, refreshments (if offered) and more.

This unique event has a two-fold benefit: you are engaging corporate decision makers in the life of your organization and you can generate special event revenue from those who sign up for the tour.

GETTING A BUSINESS SOLICITATION EFFORT UP AND RUNNING

Plan for Success With Business Prospects

What are you doing to maximize success when it comes to soliciting support from the business community? Whether you use a particular prospect management software or a form such as the example shown here, your time and ultimate success will be best used by planning and prioritizing anticipated calls on businesses.

The process of identifying key players, discovering a company's recent history of giving, determining any existing links to your organization and more, will increase your odds for success as you map out a plan of research, cultivation and solicitation.

You might even consider forming a business advisory council made up of volunteers familiar with your business community to review names and make calls on businesses capable of making generous gifts. A form similar to this would be helpful in providing ongoing direction to your most capable volunteers.

Business Prospect Profile & Anticipated Moves Schedule

Name of Business _____

Address _____

City _____ State _____ ZIP _____

Company Contacts	Titles	Phone
_____	_____	_____
_____	_____	_____
_____	_____	_____

Known Gift Recipients	Approximate Date	Gift Use
_____	_____	_____
_____	_____	_____
_____	_____	_____

Matching gift company?   ❏ Yes   ❏ No
Published gift/grant guidelines?   ❏ Yes   ❏ No
Formal gifts committee/process?   ❏ Yes   ❏ No

Links to our organization:
1. _____   3. _____
2. _____   4. _____

Likely gift/sponsorship opportunities based on what we know today:
1. _____   3. _____
2. _____   4. _____

Anticipated plan for introduction:

Who	When	Objective
_____	_____	_____

Anticipated cultivation moves:

When	What	By Whom
_____	_____	_____

Target amount: $_____

Anticipated solicitation:

When	Gift Use	By Whom
_____	_____	_____

GETTING A BUSINESS SOLICITATION EFFORT UP AND RUNNING

How to Find the Best Corporate, Foundation Prospects

The best way to gauge the interest level of a foundation or corporation — determine its capacity to give a major gift, affinity to your organization and interest in your programs, says Christina Pulawski, an independent consultant with Christina Pulawski Consulting (Chicago, IL).

"Does that corporation or foundation give its funds in the type of chunks that you need?" she says. "For example, if you need $100,000, and the foundation gives a maximum of $100,000, but in smaller amounts of $20,000, that foundation does not have the capacity to fund your project, or you will need to adjust your approach."

You can determine the prospect's affinity to your organization by looking at what ties the corporation or foundation has with your program. Do you have board members in common? Someone who can make an introduction? Are there other natural partners?

"The best organizational prospects are those with natural ties to your mission or goals, and that basically want the same outcomes your organization is trying to accomplish," she says. "They should also have an interest in your programs, and have strong ties to your community and constituency."

The goal of your initial research should be to come up with a short list of prospects, says Pulawski. "At this stage, a print-out of what your organization does with a justification of why the funder is a good match should be enough to help decide whether to move forward or invest more time in building a relationship," she says. "You will also want to involve your organization's staff to find out who among them has ties to the corporate or foundation prospects on your list.

"Remember, building strong and long-term relationships with organizational funders is just as important as building donor relationships in individual fundraising — and should be planned accordingly," she says. "Sometimes the only difference is giving motivation or the approach method."

Be Proactive About Prospect Research

General prospect research should be an ongoing, proactive activity, says Christina Pulawski, an independent consultant with Christina Pulawski Consulting (Chicago, IL).

"The ability to be proactive comes from knowing your organization — its program and needs — and who your leadership connections are, and constantly mining them for someone in their acquaintance who might have a tie to a grant-making organization," she says.

Keep an eye on organizations similar to yours and who is funding them so that you can make sure they are in the queue for an approach from you, says Pulawski.

She shares other ways you can be proactive when conducting general prospect research:

- **Build on a known relationship.** You might have a lot of grantmakers who haven't funded you to the extent of their abilities. Take a close look at who is funding your organization and where you are on their hierarchy of giving. Are you at the top or the bottom? If you are at the bottom, why are you? Is it because you have not cultivated those interests as much? You want to make sure your funders are funding you at their capacity to give to you.

- **Focus your efforts.** If you know a project needs funding — or if you anticipate general funding needs in a particular area — identify a short list of funders whose interest and capacity might lead them to consider giving you a grant or initiating a cooperative relationship.

- **Prepare and present a proposal.** Once you have a known funder and project, make sure the proposal carefully follows guidelines and has the subtleties that will click all the triggers to be a success.

Your in-depth research will take place when you are actually preparing the proposal, she says: "That's when you make the most of your database, evaluate your connections to determine the best initial approach, look at your giving history, and research your off-the-shelf material (such as foundation directories), as well as conduct a thorough analysis of the foundation or corporation's prior relationship and giving history to see how it matches up with what your funding and timing needs are."

Source: Christina Pulawski, Principal, Christina Pulawski Consulting, Chicago, IL. Phone (773) 255-3873. E-mail: c-pulawski@comcast.net

GETTING A BUSINESS SOLICITATION EFFORT UP AND RUNNING

Create a Policy for Accepting Corporate, Naming Gifts

When a nonprofit accepts a major naming gift or enters into a marketing co-venture with a company, the name of the nonprofit becomes linked with its partners, and any negative press and impressions of that company will affect the nonprofit, says Theresa Nelson, principal, Theresa Nelson & Associates (Oakland, CA).

Nonprofits should enter into such a partnership only after a rigorous, objective process to create a gift acceptance policy outlining the criteria that must first be met, Nelson says. That criteria should include whether the company is a good fit with the nonprofit's mission; what would be required of your organization; and a risk analysis.

"You need to ask yourselves, 'Will this corporate naming opportunity put us at high risk for negative publicity?'" she says. "Above all, you need to protect your own interests. You need to have an escape clause in case the company brings bad publicity to your organization. When something hurts the identity of your organization, it turns away donors and affects your reputation and ability to raise funds."

Address the issue of major corporate naming before it comes a reality, says Nelson, because once you have one group excited about a gift, and one group opposed, the question changes from whether you will accept naming gifts from companies at all, to "Do we like this company?" That can become a very heated issue.

Other areas to address in a corporate gift acceptance policy, she says, include:

- Any exceptions, e.g. corporations that you would never take donations from under any circumstances.

- Levels of recognition.

- What permanent naming privileges to offer, or if you should even offer naming opportunities to corporations.

"Organizations can normally easily determine companies they would always take gifts from and those they would never take gifts from," says Nelson, "but it's the ones in the middle that require some thought — and a gift acceptance policy."

Source: Theresa Nelson, Principal, Theresa Nelson & Associates, Oakland, CA. Phone (510) 420-0539. E-mail: nelsontm@pacbell.net

Make the Most of Your Chamber of Commerce Connections

Your local Chamber of Commerce can serve as a great resource for fund development, allowing networking opportunities that can eventually result in new and increased gifts.

Here are some of the ways you can take advantage of your chamber membership:

- Attend chamber functions (meetings, after-hours events) to meet new people and network with existing donors and volunteers.

- Make one-on-one contacts with chamber members and even those who advertise through your chamber but may not be members.

- Host a chamber-sponsored open house at your nonprofit to provide tours and make business contacts more aware of your programs and services.

- Ask chamber leadership to sponsor a program or event on your nonprofit's behalf.

- Ask chamber officials to occasionally include an article about your organization or your calendar of events in their newsletter.

To connect with your chamber, visit the U.S. Chamber of Commerce directory: www.uschamber.com/chambers/directory/default.htm

Identify Generational Businesses

Recognize that a prosperous business passed down over two or more generations may represent enormous wealth.

One measurement of inherited wealth can be derived by researching a deceased person's will and inventory, which are public documents that can be found at the county courthouse.

Local historical books found at your local library can also provide family background information and their rise to prominence.

These and other resources can help you identify and reach out to individuals and families with both financial means and a vested interest in your community's success.

GETTING A BUSINESS SOLICITATION EFFORT UP AND RUNNING

Build Relationships With Corporate, Foundation Funders

Whether introducing yourself to a foundation program officer or seeking to strengthen a relationship with a corporate giving director, use every means possible to make new introductions and strengthen existing relationships, just as with individual donors.

To create and build relationships with those who can influence your grant request:

- Send an introductory letter stating your intention to arrange an appointment.

- Attend conferences that foundation and corporate gift officers attend.

- Contribute to specialized publications they read.

- Invite them to your events.

- Ask corporate contacts for a tour of their workplace.

- Ask potential funders to speak to your organization or group of nonprofit representatives.

- Join and participate in civic organizations they belong to.

- Share news clippings on topics they are interested.

- Introduce them to individuals they would like knowing.

- Ask them to serve on a committee, task force or your board.

Don't Overlook Small Businesses for Support

Do you have focused fundraising strategies in place aimed at your area's small businesses? Recent studies indicate that this sector of the economy is on the rise.

Here are some specific actions you might take to build relationships with and support from small businesses:

- ✓ Form a business advisory committee made up of local business owners to explore common interests between your organization and area businesses.

- ✓ Sponsor a monthly program that brings area business owners to your campus or facility for educational or other events of interest to them.

- ✓ Secure a challenge grant that will match all new and increased gifts from small businesses.

- ✓ If you have an annual awards program of some sort, consider the appropriateness of including a small business of the year award.

- ✓ Create a gift category (Business & Industry) that recognizes gifts from businesses and includes accompanying benefits geared toward their interests.

- ✓ Explore partnership opportunities with small businesses.

Multiple Challenges Spur Campaign Giving

Officials at St. Olaf College (Northfield, MN) raised more than $33.1 million in cash and pledges for a new science and mathematics building in its Beyond Imagination campaign that ended Feb. 21, 2008, seven months earlier than they anticipated.

One key to the campaign's success? The use of multiple challenges to encourage gifts from various groups, says Ron Bagnall, senior director of development.

One of those challenges, made by the 3M Foundation, raised more than $784,000 by encouraging employees and retirees of 3M with St. Olaf connections to make gifts to the campaign. Under the 3 to 1 challenge, the foundation matched the first $150,000 and then went even further, matching 1 to 1 gifts that exceeded the $150,000 fundraising goal and providing an additional $50,000 for meeting the challenge.

"Co-chair John Benson, a retired executive with 3M, was invaluable in opening the door and assembling a small committee to get the word out and solicit support from key donor prospects at 3M," Bagnall says.

Another challenge, made by an anonymous donor in December 2007, consisted of a 1 to 1 match, up to $3 million, of any new or increased gifts. The donor gave them an additional $500,000 for meeting the challenge.

"This challenge sparked a fire, allowing us to finish the campaign earlier than anticipated," says Bagnall. "Several board members increased their gifts as a result of the challenge." New donors also stepped up to help fill in mid-level donations, he says, noting that many of the gifts were $100,000-plus, with a few $25,000 gifts.

Source: Ron Bagnall, Senior Director of Advancement, St. Olaf College, Northfield, MN. Phone (507) 786-3859. E-mail: bagnall@stolaf.edu

GETTING A BUSINESS SOLICITATION EFFORT UP AND RUNNING

Advice on Researching Private Companies

How do you identify and research entrepreneurs who have the potential to help your organization?

"Think about your organizational makeup and how you can engage entrepreneurs," says Laura Solla, independent prospect research consultant, Prospect Research & Development Strategies (Freeport, PA). "By definition, entrepreneurs are risk takers. They fall into every age group, some have little business experience while others have decades and they typically own their own business."

When researching entrepreneurs who own their own companies, be aware of certain issues: "Entrepreneurs often own private companies, which are the most difficult to research. Additionally, since private companies may self-report their earnings we may not understand everything that went into composing their numbers so be careful about making assumptions," says Sarah Cadbury, director of prospect research, La Salle University (Philadelphia, PA). Cadbury recommends: local business journals; your local paper's business section; a business school; and annual lists of best companies to work for, best private companies, fastest growing companies, etc.

How do you research entrepreneurs if your organization doesn't have the resources to purchase various publications or a powerful tool such as Lexis Nexis or run a database screening? "Don't discount your local public library," says Maggie Turqman, senior research librarian, National Geographic Society (Washington, DC). "Many public libraries have access to various databases and your library card and a good reference librarian are all you need to find the information you want." In addition to examining the library's publications, Turqman advises, monitor who is winning grants and awards in certain fields. "You can tell who the up-and-comers are by the grants and contracts they may be awarded for their research." She recommends using the advanced functions in a search engine to begin basic research, including news searching.

Although this is the information age, nothing can replace grass-roots relationship building, says Solla. She encourages development officers to reach out to volunteers and board members. "Research is an essential part of the development process, but it's networking and relationship building that help you identify the right individuals to engage."

Finally, don't think of all entrepreneurs as wealthy. "They may not be able to make a major gift right away and there is no guarantee they will be successful," says Cadbury. Instead, think of entrepreneurs as expansion partners in relationship building for your organization.

*Source: Laura A. Solla, Independent Prospect
Research Consultant, Prospect Research & Development Strategies,
Freeport, PA. Phone (724) 295-0679.
E-mail: Solla@ResearchProspects.com
Sarah Parnum Cadbury, Director of Prospect Research, La Salle
University, Philadelphia, PA. Phone (215) 951-5144.
E-mail: cadbury@lasalle.edu
Maggie Turqman, Senior Research Librarian, National Geographic
Society, Washington, DC. Phone (202) 857-7057.
E-mail: mturqman@ngs.org*

Turning to Business for Support: How to Increase Gift Support from Businesses & Corporations

APPROACHING BUSINESSES FOR FIRST-TIME GIFTS

To broaden your base of business support, you will need to generate far more first-time gifts from businesses. Once those initial gifts have become a reality, you can work at building a habit of giving. But first things first. This chapter will offer guidance and ideas on what you can do to make new connections and aim for expanding your list of first-time business contributors.

Four Tips to Connect With Corporate Decision Makers

Making that first contact with a business or corporate decision maker can be a challenge. And while a confirmed appointment does not guarantee a gift, the lack of one can certainly diminish likelihood of support. Turn to these techniques to gain entrance to decision makers:

1. If possible, have a mutually respected contact set the appointment and make an introductory visit with you.

2. If making contact on your own, send a brief letter two weeks prior to attempting the appointment. The letter should introduce yourself and explain the purpose of your visit. Call within a few days to set date and time.

3. After contacting the decision maker's assistant, don't simply ask to speak to the decision maker; offer your name first: "Hello, this is Jane White. May I speak with Mr. West?" This gives the impression that you already know Mr. West, improving your likelihood of getting through.

4. If you wrote the decision maker in advance, informing him/her that you would be calling, try this approach: "Hello, this is Jane White. May I please speak to Mr. West? He should be expecting my call."

Be Prepared for First-time Visits

Your odds of getting off to a positive start with a business — and securing that first-time gift — will be far better if you've done your homework and know as much as possible about the business you're about to approach.

What should you know about a business before approaching it? Here are some helpful questions you should try and answer in advance:

- Who have they been giving to in the past?
- How much does the company give away annually?
- Does the company have particular philanthropic interests?
- Who is in charge of giving decisions?
- Is there a contributions committee? How often does it meet?
- Does the company provide guidelines for gifts?
- Does the company have a history of sponsoring special programs or events? What do these include?

Attract First-time Business Donors

Want to get more businesses giving to your charity? Begin by identifying a service or product they offer that could be contributed as a gift-in-kind. Businesses view gifts-in-kind as less costly and they will involve the business in your organization and begin a habit of giving that will lead to cash gifts.

Corporate Advice

Before knocking on corporate doors for support, do some legwork. Establish definite targets for prospects whose standards for giving match your reasons for asking. Then determine the best way of approaching each prospect with a proposal that meets their interests.

Work to Land First-time Gifts From Businesses

Want to get more gifts from members of the business community? Create gift opportunities designed to get them on board. To secure more first-time gifts from businesses:

1. Share a menu of wide-ranging sponsorship opportunities. Offer a variety of sponsorship price tags.

2. Form a committee of existing business contributors to assist in identifying and calling on their colleges.

3. Launch a business partners program that includes any business contributing $250 or more per year. Offer members some exclusive benefits to attract their participation.

4. Convince an existing business donor to establish a challenge gift aimed at non-donor businesses. Any first-time gift will be matched by the challenger.

APPROACHING BUSINESSES FOR FIRST-TIME GIFTS

Set the Stage for Cold Calls With an Introductory Letter

Veteran development professionals will tell you that the best method for making contact with new prospects is through a mutual introduction by someone close to both the business/corporation and your organization. As helpful as that method can be, there are obviously times when that cannot occur. In those instances, it's better to attempt a cold call than to make no contact at all.

When it's necessary to make a cold call on a prospect, is it best to show up unannounced, hoping to gain an audience? Or should you attempt to set an appointment first? While there may be some exceptions to the rule, setting an appointment is generally the wisest move. After all, if the business in question has absolutely no interest in meeting you, it's a waste of their and your time to make the attempt.

Before calling for an appointment, however, it's best to send a personal letter of introduction — one that will set the stage for your upcoming call. Such a letter will make the case for your visit and generally improve your odds of securing an appointment. Additionally, a letter of introduction will add credibility to you and the cause you represent.

Develop a letter of introduction similar to the example at right as a first step in attempting to set an appointment with the new prospect.

Dear <Name>:

I am writing with the hope that you will give me 30 minutes of your time to introduce myself and visit with you about The Boys and Girls Home and its role in our community.

I know that your business has a long and successful history in our community and I respect the level of involvement and leadership you have taken in community affairs over the years. The Boys and Girls Home has also had a long history of service to this community, and, for that reason, I believe you and I have some mutual interests.

While it is my genuine hope that you consider a contribution to The Boys and Girls Home, I ask that you meet with me briefly regardless of any decision regarding a gift. I want you to be aware of some of the exciting achievements our organization is making, and ask for your input regarding a future project we are exploring.

I will contact you within the next 10 days to arrange an appointment. Thank you in advance for granting me this opportunity to meet with you.

Sincerely,
<Name>

Gifts-in-kind Can Lead to Cash Gifts

Keep this thought in mind: sometimes it's smarter to ask a potential contributor for something other than money. Asking a prospect for a gift-in-kind that may not be perceived as costly is one way to begin to build a relationship with a donor — and a habit of giving — that will one day lead to cash gifts.

Review your list of non-donor businesses. Ask yourself what each business offers or manufactures or sells that you could use. A service? A product? Their employees' time? Specialized know how? Then approach the business with a legitimate request for how a gift of that service, product or know how could genuinely benefit your cause.

You will find that this approach tends to be less threatening to some businesses — and more affordable from their point of view. Plus, such gift-in-kind contributions will begin paving the way for cash contributions down the road.

Discover Who Knows Who Among Businesses

To make the most of generating new gifts from businesses, it helps to know who knows who. Use those peer relationships as relationship-building entrées.

Here's a sampling of networking actions you can take to learn more about business community connections:

- Become active on a Chamber of Commerce committee.
- Form a business advisory committee made up of business representatives already supporting your cause.
- Host a golf fundraiser and observe who signs up as foursomes.
- Discover companies' vendors.
- Review newspapers, business journals.

APPROACHING BUSINESSES FOR FIRST-TIME GIFTS

Offer Businesses Choices for Giving

When calling on a business, especially one that has no prior involvement with your nonprofit, don't simply ask for a gift. Go beyond to offer a menu of options that may result in multiple types of gifts. Here's a proposed script to get you started:

Development Officer: "In addition to telling you more about our agency and its programs, I want to share some ways your business can really help us make a difference in the lives of those we serve. Specifically, I want to invite you to consider four types of involvement: 1) sponsoring one of many programs or events; 2) making an outright gift that would support our organization's work; 3) exploring gifts-in-kind; or 4) partnering with us on a program of mutual interest."

Offering multiple options gives the business an opportunity to choose those it considers most attractive. It's more difficult to say no to choices than a simple request for a gift. And who knows, some businesses may choose all four options.

> "Think about what your organization has to offer a particular business. Do you offer services that could be used by the company's employees? Could a partnership between your organization and a specific company help that firm sell more products or reach new customers?"

Treat New Businesses with Respect

What do you do when a new business opens? Try to be the first to solicit its owner or manager for a gift?

Why not distinguish your organization from the rest by taking special steps to establish a positive long-term relationship rather than running the risk of offending them with a premature ask?

Here are some steps you can take to build a positive relationship with a newly established business:

- Have employees of your organization on hand for the business' grand opening. Wear name tags that identify the organization you represent.

- Send a personal letter of welcome to the new business' CEO with no strings attached.

- Host a quarterly breakfast or lunch for community newcomers. Use the occasion to provide a tour of your facilities and offer guests a small memento.

- If the business executive is new to your community, offer to schedule some time to take him/her around and make introductions to some of the community's leaders. (Doing this also gives you an opportunity to be seen by other key prospects as well.)

- Again, if the person is new to the community, take him/her as a guest to one of your local civic club's meetings.

Business Advisory Council Helps Multiply Business Gifts

Why should you take precious time to form a business advisory council? Because council members' willingness to become involved can increase business gift revenue dramatically.

If you're just getting started, begin by reviewing your existing list of business and corporate contributors. If you want to form a group of up to 10 individuals who will meet quarterly, identify 20 prospective members — knowing your request to become involved will be declined by some — and prioritize them according to who you think would make the best council members. Then, develop a written job description for the group and begin setting individual appointments to make your case and share your written expectations.

Here are some duties your business advisory council members can take on once the group is formed:

- Review lists of current donors and agree to make individual thank-you calls.

- Review lists of nondonors and divvy out calls.

- Plan a golf classic aimed at business in your community.

- Provide insight into companies' top management and who calls the shots when it comes to contributions.

- Invite business prospects as guests to some of your charity's functions.

- Design cultivation strategies for businesses capable of major gift support.

- Host monthly power breakfasts that include a brief program on behalf of your organization.

- Help identify sponsorship opportunities for your charity's programs and match them with potential sponsors.

- Promote your cause to the public through their own businesses (i.e. notices with bank statements, store front posters, promotions that give a percentage of sales to your charity).

Although the business advisory council may describe a wide variety of possible duties, focus the group on the top two or three tasks that will provide them with a true sense of accomplishment as they complete their first year.

APPROACHING BUSINESSES FOR FIRST-TIME GIFTS

Involve Businesses in Your Nonprofit

We're all looking for ways to increase both existing gifts and the number of new donors to our institutions. But to do that, we need to strengthen existing friendships and begin establishing new ones.

To meet that challenge, begin exploring ways of cultivating relationships with businesses. Look at business cultivation just as you would the cultivation of an individual.

Identify year-long strategies that not only introduce your organization to the business, but bring that business closer to the realization of a gift. Here are some examples of business cultivation strategies that will begin resulting in increased or first-time gifts.

- Host a series of open houses for targeted businesses. Provide a tour of your facility along with a brief presentation on the impact of your nonprofit on the community, state or region.

- Target a select number of top company executives to participate in an Executives in Residence program. Identify the executive's skills that could be of value to your clients and employees. Have the executives provide a series of lectures or group discussions at your facility. The very act of getting together for sessions will familiarize the executive with your organization and begin to involve him/her with what your nonprofit is all about.

- Depending on what type of nonprofit you represent, consider establishing an ongoing Adopt A Client or Adopt A Program strategy that allows and encourages businesses to become involved with some aspect of your nonprofit on an ongoing basis.

In most cases, it's wise to establish a pattern of annual gifts from businesses before seeking a major gift. These and other strategies will initiate that process.

Locate and Attract Entrepreneurs to Your Organization

Successful entrepreneurs find a niche in the marketplace that needs to be filled and often make decisions in a short amount of time. Keep this pioneering spirit in mind when approaching an entrepreneur for a major gift, says Lisa M. Dietlin, president and CEO, Lisa M. Dietlin & Associates (Chicago, IL).

So where do you look for entrepreneurs who may be your next major donors?

If your organization is constituent-based, Dietlin says, search your database for titles such as president, CEO, founder or chairman.

If you have no built-in constituency, look for community listings such as the 500 fastest-growing businesses, largest minority-owned businesses, largest women-owned businesses, largest real estate companies, etc. In Dietlin's home base of Chicago, the publication Crain's Chicago Business compiles and posts several such lists.

Another place to find entrepreneurs is your local Chamber of Commerce. Tap and cross reference the chamber's list of businesses with your organization's databases for names of persons to contact one on one, and also arrange to make a presentation to all chamber members about the important work your organization does.

Source: Lisa M. Dietlin, President & CEO, Lisa M. Dietlin & Associates, Chicago, IL.
Phone (773) 772-4465. E-mail: info@lmdietlin.com

Content not available in this edition

APPROACHING BUSINESSES FOR FIRST-TIME GIFTS

Develop a Routine for Setting Appointments

It's so easy to get caught up in administrative demands — internal meetings, paperwork, etc. — that staff may often give less attention to making sponsorship calls than anticipated. To ensure you get out of the office on a regular basis, develop a procedure that ensures you are making a minimum number of calls every week.

Here is one example of how to set aside time for scheduling appointments:

Earmark every Tuesday and Thursday afternoon for appointment-setting. Let others know that this time is off limits for meetings and unscheduled visits. Review your list of business prospects and schedule phone calls to get appointments locked up for the next two-week period. Try to protect your Tuesday and Thursday afternoons so they will remain available as future appointment-setting periods.

By having two designated times per week for setting appointments, you will have two opportunities to attempt to reach prospects should you be unable to reach them the first time. Also, should something unexpected prevent you from scheduling calls on one of those two times, you still have a last opportunity to do some scheduling.

Map Out a Three-year Plan for First-time Donors

Plans to acquire and retain first-time donors should be based on a three-year plan:

Year 1 — Acquire first-time gifts. Develop a set of fundraising strategies aimed at acquiring first-time gifts through targeted direct mail appeals, personal visits and more. Have special cultivation strategies in place to let these donors know how much their support means to your nonprofit.

Year 2 — Focus on retaining those first-time donors rather than increasing their level of support. Since the goal should be to build a habit of giving, develop strategies aimed at reinstating those gifts.

Year 3 — Although retention should continue to be your primary focus, some donors may consider increasing support by the third year. To upgrade their level of giving in year three, ask for an unrestricted gift earlier in the year and another gift later on that's restricted to a particular funding project.

As you identify business prospects to approach, know the work affiliations of your donors, board members and volunteers. If someone affiliated with your organization is also affiliated with a specific company, that company may give grants where its employees volunteer, match employee contributions or provide volunteers you could use.

Turning to Business for Support: How to Increase Gift Support from Businesses & Corporations

FORGE RELATIONSHIP-BUILDING PARTNERSHIPS

It's all about building relationships — hopefully long-term relationships — with decision makers, with those in upper management and even with employees of businesses. Get to know your area's businesses, and enable them to get to know your organization. Treat each business relationship just as you would one with an individual. Listen and learn what matters most to them. Then tailor involvement and investment opportunities to each business or corporation.

Don't Confine Yourself to Once-a-year Calls on Businesses

Have you ever gotten this response when calling on a business? "The only time I hear from you is when you're asking me for money."

You're not alone. It happens to lots of development officers who are expected to make so many calls that it becomes challenging to have contacts with businesses beyond the normal once-a-year ask. But even so, there are actions you can take to nurture your organization's relationship with business donors and donor hopefuls.

Here's a sampling of some of the cultivation (and stewardship) moves you can take between solicitation calls:

✓ Make mention of a group of business supporters every time your internal newsletter is distributed. Then send a copy of it to the business with a note saying: "Our employees know you're an investor here, and they appreciate it!"

✓ Clip news items of interest and send them to your business contact along with a personal note: "Just thought you might find this to be of interest...."

✓ Hold one or more invitation-only receptions at your facility during the year for both business contributors and prospects.

✓ Ask board members and development committee volunteers to begin making thank-you calls on business contributors two or three months prior to your annual solicitation call.

✓ Send a midyear note or make a midyear phone call pointing out how that business' gift is making a difference for those you serve.

Six Ways to Nurture Corporate Partner Relationships

Could your organization benefit from corporate partnerships? Could those partnerships lead to more gift revenue? Then make a note of these recommendations from Jody Fidler, associate director of corporate development for The Maritime Aquarium (Norwalk, CT):

1. Seek out people who have an intimate connection to your organization. Once you make contact, invite them to tour your facility, give them one-on-one attention, and let them behind the scenes.
2. Strike a fine balance when it come to staying in touch and being overbearing.
3. Find out their interests and then invite them to events that are the best fit.
4. Keep an open mind when developing areas that would make them more interested and keep them involved.
5. Use your relationships with them to create new ones.
6. Keep them informed about what's going on at your organization.

Source: Jody C. Fidler, Associate Director of Corporate Development, The Maritime Aquarium, Norwalk, CT. Phone (203) 852-0700 ext. 2277. E-mail: jfidler@maritimeaquarium.org

Create a Corporate Identity That's Valued by Area Businesses

What goes around comes around. That's why, at least among area businesses, your organization should be perceived as a member of the local corporate/business community. While yours may be a not-for-profit entity, those in business are more easily sold on your cause if they recognize your economic impact. This is especially important as you look toward businesses within your community to underwrite an event/project.

What can you do to be more fully perceived as a corporate member of the community? Use this checklist to determine what additional steps to take:

❑ Become an active member of the local Chamber of Commerce, attending events and getting involved with various committees.

❑ Be attuned to local issues and ways in which your organization might respond to community needs that are in line with your mission.

❑ Spell out ways in which your organization positively impacts the local or area economy — number of employees, total payroll, how your presence saves taxpayers and more.

❑ Conduct business locally to the degree possible.

❑ Be alert to opportunities in which your facilities and/or services might be more fully opened to and utilized by the community.

FORGE RELATIONSHIP-BUILDING PARTNERSHIPS

Aim Your Sights at Upper Management

We're often so focused on the company CEO that we lose sight of the massive giving potential of those persons who surround a company's top official.

Individuals within upper management should be considered viable prospects for several reasons: many receive high salaries, have contacts with other higher ups and possess the ability to get things done and to influence company decisions.

Employ these strategies to involve and build relationships with persons in upper management positions:

✓ Assign someone to research your community directory and other resources, adding names and addresses of corporate vice presidents and company officers to your mailing list.

✓ Explore ways to cultivate and involve spouses of upper management personnel.

✓ Identify corporate executives who have an existing relationship with your organization. Meet with them one on one to formulate cultivation strategies aimed at upper level professionals within their respective companies.

✓ Establish a business and corporate advisory committee made up of people who are already committed to your nonprofit. Meet regularly with the group to develop cultivation strategies and programs.

✓ Establish a corporate executive of the month award (or multiple awards in different categories) that recognizes professionals for achievement in some area (e.g., civic involvement, professional achievement). Include all past award recipients in an ongoing society that meets at least yearly.

✓ Identify 10 key issues facing your organization's future that business and corporate involvement could impact positively. Use the challenges as a way to involve executives in your agency over a multi-year period.

✓ Form a corporate partners program with accompanying benefits for business executives who join or contribute. Provide benefits offering value to the business executive: discounts at restaurants, golf outings, tickets to events, receptions conducive to networking, etc.

✓ As part of a yearlong communications plan, incorporate profiles of key executives into your regularly published newsletter or magazine. Develop feature stories and submit news releases including upper management individuals who are engaged in your organization as volunteers, board members or donors.

Business Executives Cultivated at Awards Celebration

Looking for ways to cultivate business executives and companies in your area?

Five years ago, officials with the Boston Children's Museum (Boston, MA) created Great Friends to Kids Breakfast, an annual event that brings in operating dollars while building strong relationships with corporate donors and business executives. The event now attracts more than 500 Boston political and business leaders, with the goal of recognizing the important work being done for area children by fellow community organizations and business leaders.

Invitations are sent to key members of the corporate community and board members. Two awards are presented during the event: one in memory of a former museum trustee and one for outstanding volunteer leadership, which is given to an individual who advances the quality of life for children.

An awards committee of museum trustees and an event committee of representatives from other nonprofits, corporations and community groups plan and coordinate the event. "This makes the Great Friends to Kids Breakfast exquisitely inclusive and attractive for sponsorship from local businesses. In addition, it's a great networking opportunity for executives and community leaders," says Deborah Sinay, vice president for institutional advancement.

The Great Friends to Kids Breakfast has emerged as the museum's signature fundraiser and the organization has a three-year branding strategy to grow event attendance and revenue. "It was crucial we understood the target audience for this event," says Sinay. "We made sure this would be something companies and executives would want to sponsor by including the whole community in the celebration. Corporate America is looking for a way to give back.

"In addition to presenting the awards, children are involved in the event through artistic entertainment or other forms of creative expression."

Source: Deborah J. Sinay, Senior Vice President, Institutional Advancement, Boston Children's Museum, Boston, MA. Phone (617) 426-6500. E-mail: sinay@bostonchildrensmuseum.org

FORGE RELATIONSHIP-BUILDING PARTNERSHIPS

How Local Banks Can Help Your Fundraising Efforts

In spite of the way local banks continue to be gobbled up by nationwide institutions, those community banks still want to be perceived as involved corporate citizens. Consider the following ways of tapping into your area banks:

1. Get them to sponsor a newly launched program by underwriting part of its costs.
2. Invite them to support your annual fund efforts at an exemplary level.
3. Ask to use your local bank's lobby to promote an upcoming event or raffle a prize.
4. Ask the bank's CEO to serve on your board.
5. Ask banks to serve as a drop-off point for donations during special campaigns.
6. Include local banks as top prospects during your capital campaign.
7. Invite a trust officer to serve on your planned gifts advisory committee.
8. Partner with a bank on a special event that allows the bank's employees to volunteer their time.
9. Ask if you can include a special appeal stuffer in one of the bank's mailings.

Do You Have a Guest Experts Program in Place?

Here's an idea that nearly any type of nonprofit can adapt to cultivate relationships with major gift prospects: Create a guest experts program as a way to engage individuals in the life and work of your organization. Your experts could be business executives, artists, scholars, celebrities, teachers, consultants or others.

A guest experts program not only cultivates a relationship with would-be donors, it can help build relationships with those who benefit from the guest expert's insight.

To establish a guest experts program (or strengthen an existing program), keep these points in mind:

Timing —
- Make sure the schedule works for your guest, allowing flexibility for more time with the audience if needed.
- Schedule sessions with the expert around other events. Tie them in thematically, or draw on the added exposure to boost attendance.

Audience —
- Define your group based on what you want to accomplish with the event.
- You may want to limit the session to select groups (e.g., special guests, donors, board members) to add an element of exclusivity and interaction with the expert.
- Inviting large groups can also be beneficial, especially if sessions are styled in a lecture format. This broadens the range of exposure for your organization.
- Some sessions are more successful when they are open to the public, especially if fees can be charged to the attendees. This format focuses more on cultivating the guest expert rather than the audience.

Marketing the event —
- The formats you choose to promote the event will depend on the audience you plan to reach. In-house publications and direct mail work best for smaller groups

while traditional media outlets, such as news releases, will get the message to a larger, more diverse population.
- Make sure your brochures and programs reflect the event's quality and prestige.

Selecting the experts —
- Guests should be experts in their fields and known by those you hope to draw.
- They should be respected by their peers. If they only have niche recognition, market to that select group.
- The most important aspect of guest experts is their ability to impart knowledge that is fulfilling to everyone involved, including the guest. Prepare guest experts so they know what type of audience they will have and what will be expected of them.

Cultivation —
- If the experience is successful for the expert and attendees, the event can serve as a cultivation tool for both groups. Follow-up visits to the expert should include discussions about the impact of his/her presentation.
- These events can generate a variety of gifts such as funds to help cover future guest expert programs, grants from the expert's company, original works of art from artists, royalties from books and patents, and more.
- Except for attendance revenues, separate the solicitation process from the event. The presentation cultivates a relationship which later leads to a gift.

Annual program —
- If an event with a certain expert is successful, consider making it an annual event.
- Be on the lookout for future experts within and outside your donor constituency.
- Keep the quality level high, and establish it as a prestigious honor. This will help with the cultivation aspect of the process.

FORGE RELATIONSHIP-BUILDING PARTNERSHIPS

Partner With Local Businesses

When seeking vendors and sponsors, choosing local businesses can save time and money while creating opportunities to barter services for publicity.

"As a nonprofit with a very limited geographic range and which strives to promote a strong community image, it is very important to us to try to do as much work with local businesses as possible," says James Hood, communications coordinator, The Lake George Association, Inc. (Lake George, NY).

"There's something to be said for the value of more personalized service that local businesses can provide," Hood says. "When I have a rush job or sudden change that requires immediate turnaround, local businesses bend over backward, almost always with no additional cost. Local vendors are also more able to spot potential problems and alert us before we end up with a full-blown, high-cost crisis situation."

Consider offering event sponsorship in exchange for services, he says. "For example, we're planning to redesign our website. It's something that we've wanted to do for a few years, but haven't been able to find the money. We're now working with our local Web design/hosting company to get this much-needed project done at a price we can afford. We've come to an agreement that a certain amount of the job cost will be covered through a trade for the same amount in event sponsorship."

While offering vendors sponsorship opportunities can be mutually beneficial, Hood cautions against making it appear that your organization is an advertising vehicle for the sponsor. Public recognition for such donations must be done tastefully and appropriately with no favoritism or bias.

"When providing recognition to sponsors, we limit it to just that: recognition. We are publicly recognizing that they are supporting our work through a sponsorship," says Hood. "If it feels like you are starting to get into advertising, then don't do it. Your organization's public image is far more valuable than any single sponsorship."

Source: James Hood, Communications Coordinator, The Lake George Association, Inc., Lake George, NY.
Phone (518) 668-3558, ext. 301.
E-mail: jhood@lakegeorgeassociation.org

Partnership With an Unpopular Business

Do you have businesses in your community that could stand to improve their images — law firms, manufacturers or others?

If the existence of a poor image is clear to the business' top management, and they want to improve it — it's not your role to convince them — there may be mutual benefits for your organization and theirs by forming an alliance.

Meet with officials of the unpopular business to explore project possibilities that can enhance their organization's image and raise funds for your agency. Your menu of choices might include:

- A special fundraising event sponsored by the business.
- Use of their facilities or equipment by your organization.
- A public pledge that the business intends to donate a specific amount of employee time toward volunteer efforts with your organization.
- A commitment to offer their company services to your organization at no cost.

Be sure your proposal includes tangible benefits — number of news releases, television and radio opportunities, sponsorship signage and incentives for participation,.

Launch a Business of the Month Initiative

To cultivate relationships with community businesses and corporations, make it a priority to identify a Business of the Month based on criteria established by your organization. The very act of recognizing area businesses will help establish a relationship with the selected business and make other businesses more aware of your nonprofit throughout the business community.

Use this step-by-step process as a guide in developing your own program:

1. Assemble a group of existing business donors to take on responsibility for this program: determining criteria for selection, hosting each monthly citation and more. Criteria for selection could include measures such as: taking an active role in community betterment, existence of an employee matching gift program, contributing 5 percent of pre-tax earnings to community causes, etc.
2. Encourage your business advisory committee to host a monthly reception at your facility in which members of the business community are invited to learn more about some aspect of your nonprofit's work and recognize the Business of the Month recipient.
3. Invite employees of the Business of the Month to attend the event and provide them with a tour of your facilities.
4. Develop a publicity procedure to follow each time a new Business of the Month recipient is named: press release, feature in your nonprofit's newsletter/website, etc.
5. Award a plaque to the company's CEO and mementos to its employees.

FORGE RELATIONSHIP-BUILDING PARTNERSHIPS

Build Business Alliances

As you work to build relationships with businesses, exhaust every opportunity to forge alliances with employees who work for those companies. They may be helpful at influencing their company's top decision makers.

To network with as many company employees as possible use these tips:

1. Don't miss an opportunity to make a presentation or offer a facilities tour to a group of company employees.

2. Explore the feasibility of having news of your organization and its work placed in the company's newsletter.

3. Meet with those company employees who are already committed to your cause and form an ambassador committee, charging them to help speak on your behalf to colleagues.

Find the Common Cause Between Your Nonprofit and Retailers

Now more than ever, for-profit retail corporations operate with an eye toward social and environmental consciousness. Keep this in mind as you seek to add major sponsors and increase brand awareness.

At the Waikiki Aquarium (Honolulu, HI), staff have begun offering tailored partnerships with locally based small businesses and national corporations with local outposts in and around Honolulu, says aquarium representative Tess Staadecker.

Brainstorming about which for-profit organizations would make good partners led staff to Whole Foods and elle Couture Jewellers. The aquarium formed the partnerships this spring and quickly saw results, enjoying its best spring ever.

At the Whole Foods in Kahala, HI, as at most Whole Foods nationwide, shoppers receive five cents for each reusable grocery bag they bring into the store for their shopping. Beginning in April 2009, shoppers at the Kahala store could donate that five cents to the aquarium's stewardship of marine resources. Plans are to renew the program through March 2010.

For the other business partnership, aquarium staff tapped elle Couture Jewellers, which offers a sea life pendant collection from Roberto Coin. To kick off World Oceans Day on June 8, the jeweler agreed to donate 10 percent of proceeds from sales of this collection to the Friends of Waikiki Aquarium. The partnership continued through 2009 and company representatives anticipated raising $5,000 for the aquarium.

Source: Tess Staadecker, Account Executive, Waikiki Aquarium, University of Hawaii-Manoa, Honolulu, HI. Phone (808) 923-9741. E-mail: tess@beckercommunications.com

Get Businesses to Support Your Cause

A system for establishing community partnerships opens support-generating avenues.

In March 2007, The Character Education Partnership (CEP) of Washington, DC, launched a program forming partnerships with companies that had a similar mission. The purpose: to raise additional funds while forming lasting community partnerships to generate support from area businesses.

"We identify companies that emphasize character, morality, ethics and education," says Lee MacVaugh, director of development and fundraising. "We look at their mission statement, vision statement, website and advertisements for a common connection."

Examples of such partners include companies that work with schools, community groups (e.g., Boys Club) and volunteer organizations that emphasize service learning, volunteering and sponsorship of students, schools or classrooms. Companies partnered with CEP include Prudential Financial and McGraw-Hill Education.

As a part of the partnership, CEP receives sponsorship dollars for such forums as their national forum on character education and in-kind donations (e.g., computers, office space, textbooks). In return, businesses are provided opportunities such as tapping into CEP's mailing list and networks, a platform at CEP's national forum to sell products, and professional development and training for their code of ethics conduct.

To date, CEP has acquired six business partners, with hopes of establishing 15 partnerships by December. CEP has realized $85,000 in financial support through sponsorships and an additional $5,500 from in-kind gifts.

Source: Lee MacVaugh, Director of Development and Fundraising, The Character Education Partnership, Washington, DC. Phone (202) 296-7743, ext. 14. E-mail: lmacvaugh@character.org

Turning to Business for Support: How to Increase Gift Support from Businesses & Corporations

CULTIVATING YOUR NONPROFIT'S VENDORS

Although your organization's selection of business vendors should generally not take past contributions into consideration, the reverse can be helpful in the solicitation process. Vendors present a special set of circumstances when it comes to giving. Sometimes those gifts come in the form of cash contributions. Other times they come in the form of gifts or services in-kind. Be sure you are giving your organization's vendors every opportunity to invest.

Know Who's Getting Your Business

Did your charity recently make a big purchase? Which local Realtors benefitted from having your new employees as clients? Have any employee groups sponsored a dinner or reception at a local restaurant?

While a charity's selection of business vendors should generally not take past contributions into consideration, the reverse can be helpful in the solicitation process. Knowing which businesses are benefitting from your organization and its employees (and how much) can help in the timing of a solicitation, the ask amount and even the type of gift you may chose to solicit (i.e. cash or gift-in-kind).

Invite your organization's business office and employees to help you track where and when they are doing official business. Distribute a business activity form to all employees, encouraging them to complete and return it to you each time they conduct official business.

As easy as it may be for you to periodically receive a vendor report from your business office, this more comprehensive method may pinpoint purchases/expenditures that the business office alone is unable to produce. And, it's not only the amount of the expenditure that matters; your charity's prominence in the eyes of a business may have equal or greater impact.

LANCASTER ART CENTER — Business Activity Form

Please complete this form each time you or a group of employees conducts official business in our community/region. Your willingness to keep us updated may prove valuable as we cultivate and solicit gifts.

Employee/Department Submitting Form: _____

Date Submitted: _____

Name of Business Benefitting from LAC: _____

Business Contact: _____

Approximate Amount of Purchase/Expenditure: _____

Date of Purchase/Expenditure: _____

Type of Purchase/Expenditure: _____

Number of LAC employees involved: _____

Is this a recurring purchase/expenditure? ❑ Yes ❑ No

If so, when and how often? _____

How/why did you select this business? _____

Were you satisfied with the purchase/expenditure? (Please describe)
_____
_____

Would you make a purchase/expenditure with this business again? Why or why not _____

Additional comments that might provide insight into the cultivation/solicitation of this prospect: _____
_____

Host an Annual Vendors' Event

You might think it makes more sense for local and area businesses to be wooing your organization for your business rather than vice versa. So why would you want to host an event for your vendors? Call it savvy cultivation on your part.

Here's how it might work:

1. As you complete one fiscal year and embark on another, get the list of every company who was a paid vendor of your nonprofit during the past year: plumbers, electricians, equipment providers, etc. — everyone who received a check from your agency for any reason.

2. Stage an invitation-only event for this group: a breakfast, after-hours reception, or perhaps a series of open houses to be sure everyone can attend.

3. Use the event as a friend-raising opportunity. Have someone from your finance or accounting department explain your board-approved procedures for selecting vendors, then have your CEO or some other appropriate person briefly talk about your organization's mission, services and the importance of gift support.

4. In addition to wining and dining the group, you may wish to offer facility tours and/or have someone served by your organization give a testimonial.

The completion of the event provides the perfect follow-up opportunity to calls on those businesses for support.

CULTIVATING YOUR NONPROFIT'S VENDORS

Compare Similar Vendors' Giving Histories

It's wise, from time to time, to review your organization's list of vendors to determine who is giving and who is not. It can also be useful to compare your organization's relationship with similar, perhaps competing, companies, evaluating the amount of business you give each with their level of giving to your organization. A closer review may point out that one company which gives modestly is getting the bulk of your organization's business while a competing company giving at a much higher level is receiving much less of your purchasing dollars.

While many nonprofit executives will argue that purchasing decisions should be made separately from if or how much a business chooses to contribute, there's no doubt that a vendor should be considered a viable gift prospect. And while other factors may have higher priority in your nonprofit's business decisions (i.e., price, quality of workmanship, etc.), level of gift support should at least be given some consideration.

To better evaluate similar and/or competing vendors, consider making use of a report similar to the one below on a quarterly basis.

Review and compare similar vendors' business activity and level of giving.

QUARTERLY VENDOR REVIEW

For Period Ending _____   Distribute To _____

Vendor	Item/Description	Date	Amount	Gift History			
				01/02	02/03	03/04	Current
Print Vendors							
1. ABC Printing	Employee handbook	8/5/03	$1,200	$50	$50	$50	$100
2. Blue Ink Print & Design	Annual fund brochure	8/15/03	$1,744	$500	$700	$800	$1,000
Real Estate Vendors							
1. Century 21/Bill Tompson	Purchase of 30 Hardy St.	7/6/03	$7,000	—	$30	—	—
2. Nodlund/Sue Nodlund	Sale of Noddler Addition	7/10/03	$1,200	$400	$400	$400	$500
Soft Drink Vendors							
1. Semple Coca Cola Dist.	Soft drinks	8/1/03	$3,123	$2,000	$2,000	$2,000	$2,000
2. Hilman Pepsi Dist. Co.	Soft drinks	8/3/03	$1,214	$900	$1,000	$1,000	$1,250

Make Connections Through Businesses' Vendors

That tried-and-tested saying of "people don't give to organizations, people give to people," is just as true of the business community as it is of individuals.

When it comes to garnering new business and corporate support, it makes a great deal of sense to scrutinize the links existing supporters have with other businesses. Some of your donors may hold board positions; others will no doubt carry on vendor relationships with many businesses.

That's why it is worth the time to compile and maintain vendor lists for your existing business donors. With whom do each of them do business? Once you have lists in place for each supporting business, you can begin to explore those relationships and determine which, among them, hold the greatest potential of making generous gifts to your organization.

In prioritizing business' vendors as gift prospects, it's important to gauge the willingness and ability of each existing donor to help introduce your agency and assist in the solicitation process. Ask yourself in each case, "how much business does this donor do with this company? Is it

Examples of Business Vendors:

Donor	Donor's Vendors
Bread manufacturer	Distributor of flour
Automobile dealer	Newspapers, radio and television (advertising)
Printing company	Paper distributors, Printing equipment companies
Furniture store	Furniture distributors, Carpet distributors, Wall-covering distributors

considered a big account?"

You may even develop some form of rating scale to help measure the potential of each based on factors including: willingness/ability of the donor to assist in solicitation, importance of this donor's business to the vendor prospect, financial ability of vendor prospect, etc.

Look for both obvious and not-so-obvious vendor relationships as you build each list.

Turning to Business for Support: How to Increase Gift Support from Businesses & Corporations

SOLICITATION PROCEDURES

How do you go about approaching businesses and corporations for support? Do you involve peers? Do you use a team approach? What about those instances that require you to make a presentation to a corporate giving committee or a group of decision makers? Although many of the techniques used to solicit gifts from individuals applies to businesses as well, there are some differences in how to best invite businesses to invest in your cause.

Develop Solicitation Strategies for Top Prospects

You have identified a prospect you believe capable of giving $200,000 to your cause. You have introduced her to your organization, properly cultivated her and are approaching the point in the solicitation cycle of closing the gift.

How can you best plan for a successful solicitation? Who should make the ask? Who should be present? What needs to happen to ensure success?

When nearing the closing phase of a major gift request, it's wise to formulate your solicitation strategy.

Based on what you know about the prospect, first meet with key staff to outline a potential strategy and determine who should be involved in the solicitation. Then, invite those persons you deem most appropriate for the solicitation team and solicit their input as you share your solicitation outline.

This process of shaping an intended solicitation strategy with staff and then seeking volunteer input allows your volunteers to further shape an already sound plan. And by inviting their input, you engage them in owning the solicitation process.

Strategy meetings should cover topics including:

- Prospect's rating (as a major gift donor).
- Who, how and when to best set the appointment.
- Preferred time and location.
- Others who may be present or should be invited.
- Asking amount.
- Giving gap — amount the prospect has in mind.
- Strategies to close the giving gap.
- Presentation format — who says what and when.
- Uses of the gift.
- Benefits to donor.
- Materials to be shared at meeting or sent beforehand.
- Potential outcomes and responses of the request.

While this process may seem a bit daunting, rest assured that the more you use it, the easier and more natural it will become. Do so, knowing that your degree of success will be enhanced significantly by making this a regular exercise.

SOLICITATION STRATEGY WORKSHEET

Today's Date:_____

Scheduled Solicitation Date _____ Location _____

Prospect(s) _____
Rating _____
Home Ph_____ Business Ph_____
E-mail _____ Cell _____

Ask Amount *(given over time)* $_____
Giving Gap *(amount the donor has in mind)* $_____

Possible Uses of Gift *(in order of priority)*
1._____
2._____
3._____
4._____

Perceived Benefits for the Donor
1._____
2._____
3._____
4._____

Solicitor Team *(Preferably limited to three persons)*
Assigned Staff
1._____
2._____
3._____
Assigned Volunteer(s)
1._____
2._____
3._____

Additional Invitees/Attendees of Prospect
1._____
2._____
3._____

Materials Needed for Meeting
_____ ❑ Send in Advance ❑ Share at Meeting
_____ ❑ Send in Advance ❑ Share at Meeting
_____ ❑ Send in Advance ❑ Share at Meeting

Preferred Presentation Format *(who says what)*
Conversation Leader: _____
Solicitor: _____
Support: _____

Potential Outcomes
Outcome #1 _____
Response/Follow-up _____

Outcome #2 _____
Response/Follow-up _____

Outcome #3 _____
Response/Follow-up _____

SOLICITATION PROCEDURES

Offer Businesses Varied Gift Options

Wanting to broaden support from community and area businesses? Try offering different funding projects knowing some may be more appealing than others.

Whether you do it monthly or quarterly, develop a one- or two-page newsletter that includes varied funding projects each time it's sent out (or delivered) to businesses. In addition to the wish list of funding opportunities, your newsletter can include brief news items about your programs and services that may be of interest to businesses. Be sure to enclose a business reply envelope with each issue.

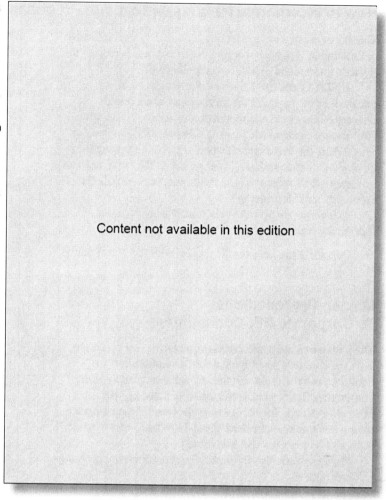

Content not available in this edition

What Should a Grant Proposal Look Like?

Most foundations provide very strict guidelines for submitting grant proposals, but what should you do if they don't?

Cheryl A. Clarke, fundraising consultant and trainer (Mill Valley, CA), says when a foundation doesn't provide any guidelines, organizations should follow this framework for organizing a proposal:

- **Intro/summary**
- **Agency history/mission**
- **Need or problem being addressed** (includes defining the constituency being served and where)
- **Outcomes** (proposed results or changes that will occur)
- **Methods** (or project description —what you are actually going to do)
- **Evaluation** (how you plan to assess the outcomes and methods)
- **Future funding** (how you plan to fund the program in the future)
- **Conclusion**

"Proposals should make a persuasive case," says Clarke. "I strongly believe in telling a good story to the funder, one that will inform as well as persuade."

Clarke says her proposal narrative are three to five pages.

Source: Cheryl A. Clarke, Fundraising Consultant and Trainer, Mill Valley, CA. Phone (415) 388-9126.
E-mail: cheryl@cherylaclarke.com

Grant Proposal Writing Dos and Don'ts

Fundraising consultant and trainer Cheryl A. Clarke (Mill Valley, CA) shares these dos and don'ts for writing grant proposals:

- Follow guidelines to the letter.
- Proofread, proofread, proofread, then get someone else to proofread.
- Never assume the reader knows about your community's need, your constituency or your agency. Be thorough and tell them.
- Do not exaggerate.
- Write in an energetic style using present tense and an active voice.
- Use simple, clear language.
- Remember you are writing to and for a real person.
- Cite primary sources when including data.
- Make all information as clear and obvious as possible.

SOLICITATION PROCEDURES

How to Incorporate Persuasive Text Into Proposals

The three critical steps to securing funding from a corporation or foundation: 1) Make your proposal stand out, 2) engage the reader's interest and 3) build a compelling case.

All three steps can be achieved through use of persuasive text, says Jessica Indrigo, senior associate director of corporate and foundation relations, Washington University School of Medicine (St. Louis, MO).

"While the beneficial effects of a proposed project may be obvious to stakeholders," Indrigo says, "they may not be clear to the funder who has read multiple proposals for seemingly similar projects."

To incorporate persuasive text into your proposals, Indrigo advises:

- Document the need for the project with facts, preferably from objective sources. "A string of adjectives is likely to be dismissed as empty hype," she says.

- Define the solution by listing the proposed project's measurable goals and describing its quantitative impact.

- Demonstrate quality of leadership, unique resources and a history of relevant accomplishments — elements that distinguish an organization from its peers.

- Convey passion for the proposed project using strong declarative verbs and an active voice.

Source: Jessica Indrigo, Senior Associate Director of Corporate and Foundation Relations, Washington University School of Medicine, St. Louis, MO. Phone (314) 935-9687. E-mail: indrigoj@wustl.edu

Making Presentations To Corporate Gift Committees

The key to making a successful presentation to a corporate gifts committee is developing a strong relationship between your nonprofit and the key decision makers at the corporation. Tailor your presentation to those key decision makers — usually the CEO and/or the head of the corporate giving committee — because if you have them on your side, it doesn't matter who else is involved.

Here are some tips for making presentations to corporate gift committees:

- Align the content of your presentation with the corporation's priorities.

- Let them know beforehand the format that you will use to make your presentation (i.e., Will you use Powerpoint? How much time will you allow for Q&A? Will you provide handouts?)

Overcome the 'You Don't Give Us Enough Business' Syndrome

If your responsibilities include soliciting local businesses for support, you've no doubt come across those who refuse to contribute based on your organization's lack of business with them. Be prepared when that happens by having a menu of responses from which to choose.

Business Prospect Objection
"The only time I see you people is when you want a handout. You know, we could use your business."

Possible Responses
"I know it's the intent of our business department to give local businesses equal opportunities to bid on projects. Let

Work at Improving Negotiation Skills

Knowing when and how to negotiate is both an art and a science. Many successful solicitations are the result of appropriately timed and thought-out negotiations.

Here are three techniques that can help you become a better negotiator:

1. Determine your position in advance of your appointment and attempt to anticipate the prospect's possible reactions so you will be prepared with counter offers.

2. Don't get so hung up on details that you lose sight of your primary objective. If, for instance, the prospect prefers to pay your requested amount over a five-year period rather than two years, be prepared to accept those conditions.

3. Pay attention to what is motivating the donor. It pays to listen. Be sensitive to what is motivating the potential gift, and use that information to close your sale. If the prospect is driven by ego, for instance, focus on those donor benefits.

me convey your concern and be sure that you're given every opportunity to make an offer next time."

"Actually, Mr. Smith, I'm not here to ask you for anything today. I simply want to update you on what our agency has been up to and to invite your input on how we can improve our services."

"I admit, Mr. Smith, there's probably a tendency for our business office to give a slight edge to those businesses that have been regular contributors. We would certainly be grateful to have you among that group of annual supporters."

SOLICITATION PROCEDURES

10 Solicitation Mistakes to Avoid

Whether you're a seasoned development professional or new to the job, avoid these 10 solicitation mistakes:

1. **Not asking.** No ask, no get. It's that simple.

2. **Not being direct.** Don't hint at what you want. Look your prospect in the eyes and make your request clear.

3. **Apologizing or begging.** Remember: making a gift is a privilege, not charity.

4. **Being unfamiliar with your nonprofit's finances.** If you're talking money, you should know about your employer's finances.

5. **Aiming too low.** Don't underestimate a donor's giving potential. Ask for more than you expect to receive.

6. **Failing to ask your own family, friends and colleagues.** If you believe in your cause, why wouldn't you approach your closest allies?

7. **Not being up-front.** Be open and honest about asking for funds.

8. **Asking only once.** Know that if a prospect says "no," it might mean "not now." Be persistent.

9. **Not asking for what you want.** If a project requires $5,000 to complete, don't ask for less. Go for it.

10. **Stopping with the first "yes."** If a donor has contributed once, don't assume that's it for the year. That should be their decision, not yours.

Don't Interpret 'No' as 'Never'

When a major gift prospect says "no" to your ask, be careful not to interpret that response as "never."

Many times the prospect is simply saying "not now." Any number of circumstances, including timing, may be an issue. Sometimes would-be donors simply aren't energized by the funding project. In that situation, you may need to focus on learning more about the individual's interests, let some time go by and then go back and make another ask.

Perfect the Art of Solicitation Small Talk

Going into a meeting with a potential donor requires plenty of preparation — and that includes preparing off-topic subjects to talk about at the start of the meeting.

"Small talk is about having knowledge of the prospect," says Jerry Smith, founder of the development consulting firm, J.F. Smith Group (Auburn, AL). Small talk, therefore, is just as important as knowing about the prospect's financial capabilities. The difference is that your prospect is much more likely to want to discuss family, hobbies, and interests than stock portfolios and bank accounts.

Every solicitation meeting should begin with small talk that is off the topic of the meeting's purpose, Smith says. "When I first started in this business, I jumped right into my presentation, which isn't very good," he says. "Small talk is really important because it's an ice breaker, and because people like to talk about themselves."

While people may think the art of small talk is a natural talent, Smith insists it is a skill set you must acquire.

The most basic information to arm yourself with for successful small talk includes the donor's marital status, the occupations of the donor and his/her spouse and where both work, children's names and their school grades.

A very easy small-talk question, Smith says, is something like, "I know Mary's in the fifth grade. How's the fifth grade going for Mary?"

To get background information on prospects, Smith says, do an online search using google.com or other search engine.

Another easy, effective way to begin small talk is to simply notice your surroundings, especially since solici-

Balance Solicitation Team

When a solicitation team includes two people, one should be able to answer questions related to the funding project and the other should be experienced at asking.

Also, don't overpower a prospect. In a major gift call, the number of solicitation team members should generally be equal to or less than the number of prospects and should rarely exceed three.

tations tend to take place in the potential donor's home or office. What are people doing in the framed photos you see? Even if they are doing something you know nothing about — say playing golf — you can always ask, "How long have you played golf?" That sort of question doesn't require any personal knowledge of golf to get a conversation going.

And if all else fails, Smith says, there is one surefire question you can ask that anyone would love to answer: "Tell me, how did you get to where you are today?"

Source: Jerry Smith, Founder, J.F. Smith Group, Auburn, AL.
E-mail: jerrysmith@jfsg.com
Website: www.jfsg.com

SOLICITATION PROCEDURES

How to Respond When Business and Philanthropy Get Mixed

How do you deal with business contacts who refuse to give because they feel your nonprofit hasn't sent enough business their way? It's a constant obstacle the development officer has to overcome. That's why you should have one or two thought-out responses in mind.

Here's an example of a local Realtor being solicited for an annual gift:

Solicitor: "I invite you to make a $250 gift to this year's annual fund effort."

Prospect: "Why should I? You folks never refer any of your new hires my way!"

Solicitor: "I can appreciate your concern. However, when it comes to new hires, we try to be as fair as possible to everyone by making no referrals to anyone. It's our hope that the decision to support our organization is based on the value of our services to the community and its residents. I do hope your final decision will be based on what we are striving to accomplish and the impact your gift has in making it happen."

Dealing With Donors Who Get the Jump On You

It's common in the fundraising profession: You approach a prospect with a figure in mind, but she beats you to the punch and offers something less than the amount you were about to suggest. Do you gracefully accept the low-ball gift? After all, it is a gift. Or do you say thanks and proceed to ask for more?

Your own experience in the field will help you gauge what works best based on individual personalities and their level of affiliation with your organization. If, however, you decide it's worth the risk of asking for more, here's one approach for articulating that message:

Scenario: You approach a local small business owner for her annual gift. She's been giving $100 a year for the past four years, and you would like to upgrade her support to $200 this year.

Donor: "I'll do what I've done in past years. Put me down for $100."

Solicitor. "First, let me point out how grateful we are for your loyal support. Without friends such as you, there's no way we would be able to accomplish some of what I just described. Having said that, I would be thrilled if you would consider a gift of $200 this year, and here's why...."

Be sure that the donor knows how important her usual gift is to your efforts. Don't belittle that in any way. And when you make the case for an increased gift, justify it with a compelling reason that the prospect can support (i.e., what you will be able to accomplish with the additional revenue, how increased costs require additional support just to maintain the current level of services, etc.)

> **Savvy Solicitation**
>
> ■ If you find yourself hesitant to suggest a specific amount when setting the stage for a major gift request, use a chart. Refer to the chart and tell the prospect, "Picture yourself among this group of donors." By giving the prospect a level rather than an amount, you can set out to negotiate a major gift commitment.

Encourage Businesses to Give Percentage of Profits

What are you doing to encourage area businesses to increase their support of local charitable causes such as yours? In some cities, business executives publicly pledge a percentage of their annual income to charity. Here are two examples:

The Two Percent Club — In Denver, members of the Two Percent Club (established in 1990) agree to donate a minimum of 2 percent of company profits to charities.

All community involvement including cash donations, employee volunteer time, in-kind goods and services, corporate volunteer projects and pro bono assistance make up the 2 percent requirement.

There are no annual dues, just a one-time registration fee of $200 to join the club. Members meet periodically to hear speakers, share ideas on charitable giving and network with others.

The club currently boasts about 150 members.

The One Percent Club — Philanthropists in Minneapolis have taken the concept a step further by pledging to give away at least 1 percent of their net worth or 5 percent of their income (whichever is greater) annually to charity.

The One Percent Club was started by local philanthropists Tom Lowe and Joe Selvaggio in 1997.

Unlike other organizations, the One Percent Club is for individuals, not corporations. Since its inception, the club has grown from 30 members to more than 1,000, and is still growing at about 12 members per month.

Almost half of the members have increased their charitable giving after joining the club, contributing more than $100 million cumulatively to charities.

For more information go to: twopercentclub.org or onepercentclub.org

Turning to Business for Support: How to Increase Gift Support from Businesses & Corporations

PROVIDE BENEFITS TAILORED TO BUSINESSES

What are you offering businesses as ways to invest in your cause? How are those benefits different from those you might offer individuals? Do the benefits you offer become more exclusive for gifts and grants at higher levels? Pay particular attention to "what's in it for me?" as you identify benefits that will most appeal to various types and sizes of businesses.

Identify Perks for Business Donors

Before approaching would-be donors, identify those benefits that will most grab the attention of businesses and those you can afford to offer. Sometimes the least expensive perks are among the most attractive to sponsors.

Develop a list of donor benefits from which you can choose as you prepare individual proposals to deliver.

Here are examples of benefits to consider including on your list:

- List donors on your website and invite clients to patronize them.

- Provide a link on your website to donors' websites.

- Host a donors' reception at your facility, including guests your donors may wish to invite.

- Send press releases to publications catering to the same readers to which your donors market. Begin by asking donors where they place their advertising.

- Include articles in your newsletter or magazine about your donors.

- Place your donors' marketing materials on display in a prominent location at your organization.

Play Up Your Most Appealing Donor Perks

Here are some benefits nonprofits are offering their corporate donors:

Make the sponsorship exclusive. Aspen Music Festival and School (Aspen, CO) promises that its corporate sponsors won't get lost in a sea of logos. One of the organization's sponsorship benefits is exclusivity by offering targeted sponsorship opportunities that provide maximum exposure for the lead sponsors.

Name drop. At the Columbus Museum of Art (Columbus, OH) $50,000-plus corporate donors get their names mentioned on the museum's 24-hour information line, which tells callers about the current exhibitions, programs and events at the museum.

Exposures count. The Preservation Society of Newport County, also know as The Newport Mansions (Newport, RI), offers its corporate donors visibility. The museum boasts more than 500,000 visitors each year. Corporate donors get their corporate name and logo on one million preservation society brochures and admission tickets, and on the organization's website, which averages one million hits per year.

Attention to employees. Minuteman Senior Services (Burlington, MA) offers its corporate donors on-site seminars for their employees on elder caregiver issues.

What About a Special Club for Business Contributors?

If generating more support from businesses is a key goal, consider a special gift club or bolstering your existing club. Just like individuals, businesses, too, like being part of an exclusive group. Consider giving businesses that make a minimum annual gift:

- Tickets to some of your events throughout the year.

- Invitations to join a special business advisory group.

- Invitations to a series of programs throughout the year

geared specifically to business interests — monthly business executives' breakfast, speakers' program, etc.

- Inclusion of its name in a special section of your annual honor roll of contributors.

- A special rate on services provided by your organization.

- A visit by your organization's CEO or board chair.

- A plaque, certificate or other memento to display as a proud supporter of your cause.

PROVIDE BENEFITS TAILORED TO BUSINESSES

Solicitation Strategies: Ask Funders to Become Partners

To be successful in soliciting gifts from funders — especially sponsors and underwriters —representatives of nonprofits need to shift their thinking from charity to partnerships and from funding to investing, says Jean Block, president, Jean Block Consulting, Inc. (Albuquerque, NM), and author of "Fast Fundraising Facts for Fame and Fortune."

This shift takes a marketing approach, Block says, and marketing has everything to do with successful fundraising: "Marketing means finding a need and filling it — if you can. It means both you and the donor need to win. One size does not fit all. You need to match your request to the funder's needs."

Rather than sending one fundraising letter with the same message to 150 funders or showing them a canned benefits package, you need to show each funder that you have researched his/her marketing needs and how you can help meet those needs, says Block.

"Once you meet their needs, they will meet yours," she says. "When you begin to think about donors as investors, you begin to think about how you can provide them with a return on investment."

This shift from selling to opportunity eliminates the need for begging or whining, says Block: "Rather than going to them with your hand out asking for a contribution, you can go to them and say, 'We have an opportunity with our organization to help you get your needs met. But before we

When Asking Funders to Be Partners, Know It Isn't About You

When soliciting gifts from prospective partners, remember it's not about you, says Jean Block, president, Jean Block Consulting, Inc. (Albuquerque, NM).

"Don't use the word 'should' when speaking to them," says Block. "It's not about what they should do, it's about the partnership."

This shift away from you begins with your printed communication pieces, says Block. "Take your annual fund letter or brochure and two different colored highlighters and with the first color, highlight all the times the letter or brochure says 'I', 'we', or your agency's name on it. With the other color, mark all the times the letter says 'you' or 'your.' You will find that there are more instances of 'I,' 'we,' or your agency's name, than 'you' or 'your.' Use 'you' and 'your' more often and focus on the benefits for your partner rather than on you."

Once you have researched what your prospective partners' needs are, you can go to them to begin to build the partnership, says Block. Start every conversation with a focus on their needs, e.g.: "I researched your website and I see that you are looking to invest in programs to improve X. I would like to bring a proposal to your attention, but first I would like to talk about your needs."

If you can invest in that kind of research before sending a board member to follow up with a prospective partner, she says, the board member can say to him or her, "When we talked, you said X. We have the perfect opportunity to do that for you."

know what that opportunity is, we need to talk.'

"If I can't use 'opportunity' when speaking in a fundraising context to a prospective funder, I know I'm not ready to talk to them."

Source: Jean Block, President, Jean Block Consulting, Inc., Albuquerque, NM. Phone (505) 899-1520. E-mail: jean@jblockinc.com

Match Partners With Appropriate Programs

Although convincing a business to partner with your organization can be challenging, your likelihood of success will increase by finding the right match between partner prospects and programs or services. To do that:

1. Identify and categorize each of your organization's programs and/or services for which you would like to find an appropriate partner. For example, a domestic violence center might define "prevention efforts" as a separate program and then work to find the right business to take on prevention as its partnership effort.

2. After identifying and categorizing particular programs and/or services, document each in the form of

partnership proposals that can be presented to partner prospects. Each proposal should include: 1) What's currently being done, 2) what you would expect of a partner in addressing that program or service and 3) the positive impact that would be realized with the partner's assistance and commitment.

3. Assemble a partnership committee of individuals who can help to identify, prioritize and approach potential partners.

This well-planned system will help attract more partners and accomplish more in matching them with appropriate programs and/or services.

PROVIDE BENEFITS TAILORED TO BUSINESSES

Match Corporate Needs to Sponsorship Level Benefits

Recognition levels for corporate donations are different than recognition levels for corporate sponsorships, says William J. Pitcher, president, Pitcher Group (Mississauga, Ontario, Canada).

"Donor benefits are about recognition. Sponsor benefits are about driving sales and other business objectives. Organizations should usually spend five times as much on sponsor benefits as on donor benefits."

The best way to determine how to provide companies with real value when creating sponsor benefits is to ask the experts — the prospective companies themselves, says Pitcher. To create sponsor benefits that are valuable to corporations, he says, organizations need to do three things:

1. Identify the company's key sales strategies.

2. Review them with the potential contributor.

3. Create an accurate and compelling proposal.

"By focusing first on the nature of a company's business and not simply on added-value bells and whistles of a request, you create opportunities with real value at their core," says Pitcher. "Creating core value will help you secure more and larger contributions."

Source: William J. Pitcher, President, Pitcher Group, Mississauga, Ontario, Canada. Phone (416) 410-6080. E-mail: william@pitchergroup.com

Content not available in this edition

Garner Business Support With WIIFM Approach

How successful are you at convincing businesses to invest in your cause?

Officials with Manteca Convention and Visitors Bureau (Manteca, CA) use the What's In It For Me (WIIFM.) strategy each time they reach out to businesses for support. "We make sure that what we are offering is helpful to the business, i.e., advertising, e-ads, etc.," says Linda Abeldt, executive director.

To identify what's meaningful to businesses, go to current business donors and seek their input. It's a great way to involve them in your organization and its work.

Source: Linda Abeldt, Executive Director, Manteca Convention & Visitors Bureau, Manteca, CA. Phone (209) 823-7229. E-mail: MTCASCVB@AOL.COM

Give Business Contributors Special Status

Create a program tailored to attracting financial support from local and area businesses.

One East Coast university created The Ambassador Club to recognize businesses giving $500 or more a year. Members attend events geared to them. Gifts have grown significantly as a result of the focused effort.

Make a yearlong commitment to host monthly events that include a brief program on topics geared to attendees' interests. Form an advisory committee to identify and offer perks that grab the attention of would-be members.

PROVIDE BENEFITS TAILORED TO BUSINESSES

Be the Best at Honoring Event Sponsors

The ways in which you recognize sponsors will not only impact their future sponsorship decisions, but also would-be sponsors.

Choose from an array of recognition actions that will help your nonprofit stand out among others. These forms of recognition may include the following;

- Special seating and public recognition at events.

- Advertisements geared toward targeted audiences.

- Feature stories on your sponsors in your own publications and in the public media.

- Perks for the sponsoring company's employees.

- Invitation to a preview party.

- Prominent recognition in all printed materials.

- Prominent signage at key locations.

- Letters of thanks from board members, your CEO, those served by your nonprofit and others.

- Evaluation interview and report following the program or event.

Recognize What's In It For the Corporate Donor

Corporate prospect research is about more than knowing how much money a corporation is able or willing to give. It's also about knowing what the corporation will get out of making a gift. So when researching a corporate prospect, remember to factor in "what's in it for them?" This information will also help you in developing your solicitation approach. Use this checklist:

- ✓ Are their consumers your donors or alumni?

- ✓ Do they recruit on your campus?

- ✓ Have they sponsored research contracts or grants?

- ✓ Have they sponsored or co-sponsored similar events for similar organizations?

- ✓ Do they serve on your board or the boards of similar organizations?

- ✓ Does their corporate volunteer and/or donation program fit with your mission?

Turning to Business for Support: How to Increase Gift Support from Businesses & Corporations

OFFER SPONSORSHIPS AS ONE VIABLE OPTION

Often sponsorships represent the best way to get new businesses on board as supporters. Whether businesses sponsor an event or a new program or some other project, don't underestimate the value of sponsorships as a way to secure support from both small businesses and larger corporations. There's no end to the list of sponsorship opportunities that may exist with your organization. Once business sponsors build a habit of loyal support, they will become much more likely to make outright gifts.

Personal Connections Help Secure Sponsorships

Each year the Friends for an Earlier Breast Cancer Test® organization (Greensboro, NC) hosts its Gathering of Friends, a fundraiser made possible through sponsorships that are, in turn, made possible through personal connections, strong presentations and appealing incentives.

Staff solicits sponsorships at several levels — $40,000 (research grant), $25,000 platinum, $10,000 gold, $5,000 silver and $2,500 bronze. Typically, two or three sponsors sign on at the highest levels and as many as 40 at other levels.

"In addition to the 'feel-good' aspect and the contribution to the greater good, there needs to be 'something in it for them' that you can offer sponsors."

"Many of our sponsorships are secured through personal relationships," says Kara McBurney, event coordinator. "We have a board of directors of local doctors, lawyers and businessmen/women who work for and are connected to major local, national and international organizations. This has been instrumental in securing sponsorships. Also, many of our sponsors have a personal connection to breast cancer."

Although the personal connections may get the organization in the door, presenting key decision makers with quality information and offering attractive incentives helps to lock in the sponsorship, McBurney says.

When Friends' founder Martha Kaley meets with potential sponsors, McBurney says, the founder discusses the history and mission of the organization, its goals, accomplishments and unique features. She also makes it known that her organization has little overhead, so approximately 80 percent of each dollar raised goes directly to research.

Additionally, Kaley presents the potential sponsor with a comprehensive solicitation piece that includes:

- Information on the fundraiser itself — logistics, sponsorship information, speaker.
- The organization's story, mission statement and founder's biography.
- Breast cancer facts.
- A historic listing of medical grants the organization has funded since 1997.
- A listing of the medical advisory board, as well as its board of directors.
- Pertinent news articles and press releases.

The presentation is not complete without offering sponsors something in return for their generosity. In addition to being reminded that they are contributing to critical medical research, sponsors are offered advertising, recognition and a tax deduction.

"It must be a win-win," McBurney says of the nonprofit/sponsor partnership. "In addition to the feel-good aspect and the contribution to the greater good, there needs to be 'something in it for sponsors.'"

Source: Kara McBurney, Event Coordinator, Friends for an Earlier Breast Cancer Test®, Greensboro, NC. Phone (336) 286-6620. E-mail: kmcburney@earlier.org

---

Sponsorship Tips

- Take full advantage of your sponsorship connections. Along with offering additional publicity for your sponsors on your organization's website, add links to your sponsors' websites as well. It's even possible that corporate sponsors could create a customized page for visitors who arrive via your website.

- Sometimes businesses like to be seen partnering with other businesses. They may see certain synergies to be gained through alliances. Explore sponsorship opportunities that may align two or more businesses.

- If your nonprofit is blessed with scores of volunteers, don't overlook the notion of offering their services as a perk to a would-be corporate sponsor for help with a one-time project — providing, of course, the volunteers buy into the idea.

OFFER SPONSORSHIPS AS ONE VIABLE OPTION

Proposals Play a Key Role in Landing Sponsorships

Big Brothers Big Sisters of Middle Tennessee (Nashville, TN) has found that putting together a significant sponsorship proposal, rather than asking for a dollar donation, generates more support from area businesses.

"For the Middle Tennessee community at least, there are so many worthy nonprofit organizations performing great tasks that the competition for philanthropic dollars is fierce," says Sarah Beatty, events manager. "By appealing to a company's marketing interests, you help them combine marketing exposure with community-minded philanthropy. You are more likely to secure sponsorship and the relationship is also more rewarding for the sponsor. They are also more likely to renew the following year and begin a true partnership."

Proposal Elements

Typical elements of a sponsorship proposal include: media exposure; logo representation on both the event Web page and the sponsor's regular website; event signage (donated); event program (try to secure in-kind sponsors for all event expenses); listing of the sponsor's physical address on your event Web page; event tickets; logo representation in e-mail blast campaigns to supporters, etc.

"Media partnerships are very beneficial, both in terms of promoting your event, but also providing exposure for the sponsor," says Beatty. "If you can get a printer to donate a program, that's a tangible print ad that attendees and participants take with them and will hopefully review at a later date."

In addition to the typical sponsorship proposal elements, she suggests that proposals be tailored to the particular company, especially if it is a major sponsor. "We ask ourselves what would appeal to them? For example, perhaps they would like to do a direct mailing to your client list (one time, and you should control it) — or an in-store campaign that highlights your partnership. Look at what the sponsor is already doing for clues."

Making the Submission

There is no perfect time to submit a sponsorship proposal, says Beatty. She has made cold calls and e-mailed over a proposal. Her CEO has presented proposals to long-term major supporters, and everything in between. "Most companies evaluate sponsorship dollars at least three months in advance, some six months, and some only once a year; so don't sit around waiting for the perfect time," she says.

Although it works best to submit a proposal in person, it is sometimes tough to get in-person meetings with busy professionals. Beatty says: "I always ask for a meeting if I think it is appropriate and then ask how they would best like to receive the information. These days, it's mostly e-mails, unless it's a company that runs proposals by a committee. On occasion, the company will ask that a hard copy be sent by mail."

Source: Sarah Beatty, Events Manager, Big Brothers Big Sisters of Middle Tennessee, Nashville, TN. Phone (615) 522-5659.
E-mail: sarah.beatty@bbbs.org

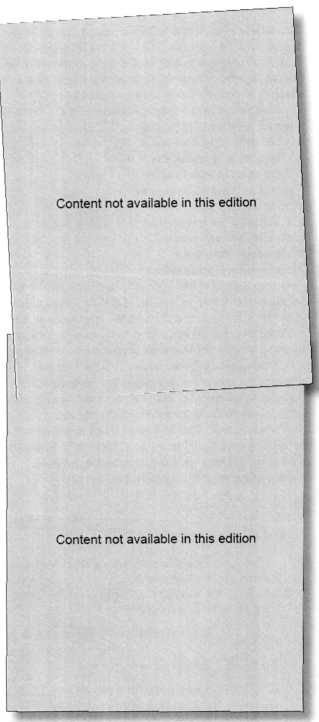

Content not available in this edition

Content not available in this edition

OFFER SPONSORSHIPS AS ONE VIABLE OPTION

Have You Considered a Sponsorship Menu?

Although you are no doubt familiar with wish lists and the ways they can be used to generate funds for needed projects, have you ever developed your own menu of sponsorship opportunities?

Much like a wish list, a sponsorship menu is a printed piece that depicts an organization's gift opportunities for businesses and individuals alike. The primary difference between a sponsorship menu and a wish list is that a sponsorship menu offers advertising opportunities. In fact, many businesses view sponsorships as advertising and, as a result, funding is generally more available than through outright gifts.

Sponsorships can be used to help underwrite existing programs or provide programming not met through a general operating budget.

Although the primary benefit to the donor is often in the form of advertising, both the organization and sponsoring donor can derive additional benefits — sponsoring company employee involvement in the event or program, an enhanced company image as a responsible corporate citizen and more.

Here's how you can develop your own sponsorship menu:

1. Evaluate all of your organization's existing programs and events. Which ones might have sponsorship appeal? A review of your institution's budget may also reveal potential sponsorship opportunities.

2. Next, brainstorm with employees to identify needs that are not presently being addressed through the budget. Which needs might demonstrate appeal as sponsored programs or events? Put yourself in the place of a would-be sponsor, and ask yourself, "Why would I be interested in sponsoring this program?" Your answer will help determine whether or not it is sponsorship material.

3. List all sponsorship opportunities together and attach a sponsor pricetag to each. Assign an overall sponsorship cost to each program or event and then look for additional sponsor opportunities

within each program.

4. After drafting a menu of sponsorship opportunities, share it with your development committee as well as a handful of nondonors. Ask for their input. What would they change, remove or add to your list? (Sharing this draft selectively will actually help pre-sell items to those involved with the process.)

5. In addition to printing the sponsorship menu, print a simple fact card for each of your larger sponsorship opportunities. Each fact card can delineate lesser sponsorship opportunities within the larger program and spell out specific benefits for the sponsor (e.g., outdoor advertising, signs at the event, pre- and post-publicity, etc.).

Below is a simple example of such a menu to guide you in creating a document that works best for you. Although a sponsorship menu could be incorporated into a direct mail effort, its greatest effectiveness will be realized through face-to-face calls.

MARENGO PUBLIC SCHOOL
2009-10 Sponsorship Opportunities

Marengo Golf/Tennis Classic

Overall sponsor	$10,000
Golf sponsor	$5,000
Tennis sponsor	$2,500
Golf clinic	$750
Tennis clinic	$250
Social hour	$500
Dinner/program	$500
Holes/tees (18)	$120 each

Theatre: Fall performance

Overall sponsor	$2,500
Program sponsor	$500
Post-performance reception	$500

Sponsor a debater

Limit of 20 ....$200 each
The sponsors of this year's debate program will help underwrite travel, lodging and meals associated with our student debate team. You will also be special guests at our Debate Invitational and meet our debaters at a special reception following the event.

For more info: Contact Betsy Swan, 282-0553

Annual lecture series

5 lectures .... $3,000 each
We will host five lectures throughout the year. This year's theme is "values worth protecting." The events are geared to students but open to the public.

Marengo career day

Event sponsor	$1,000
Career panel (5)	$250 each
Luncheon sponsor	$500

Marengo holiday performance

Overall sponsor	$2,000
Holiday reception	$500
Regional tour sponsors	$3,000 each

Marengo Band:
Fall, spring performances

Fall sponsor	$1,000
Spring sponsor	$1,000

Faculty fall retreat $5,000
Each August, Marengo faculty is invited to participate in a three-day professional development and planning session. Outside speakers and facilitators are enlisted for a productive and motivational experience.

For information about athletic sponsorship opportunities, contact Alex Martin: 282-0564

OFFER SPONSORSHIPS AS ONE VIABLE OPTION

Secure Sponsorships by Packaging All Special Events

After a few years of struggling to find sponsors for their two major fundraisers, officials with Rutland Health Foundation (Rutland, VT) decided to package their annual Bella Italia and golf invitational events in a one-time solicitation effort.

"We had two large events, live in a small community with limited prospects and were going back to the same vendors twice," says Bernadette Robin, director of annual and special giving. "On the suggestion of a volunteer committee member who is also a part of the business community, we decided to package our events, thus soliciting our prospects one time. In one mailing, our prospects are given a menu of opportunities to support one or both events."

Robin details the steps used when securing sponsorships:

1. In late October, a save-the-date card is sent to past attendees and participants of the golf event and gala dinner. "The card reminds our sponsors of the events in a light-hearted and non-obtrusive way," says Robin.

2. Committee reviews the sponsorship package to ensure it is priced appropriately and that the sponsor benefits continue to have relevance.

3. Sponsorship packages, along with a cover letter signed by the event's chair, are distributed. "The cover letter thanks past participants for their continued support and reminds them again of the value of their participation (e.g., "With your help, we were able to raise more than $30,000 for important community health initiatives…"). Recipients are reminded of their past sponsorship level and are encouraged to consider the next level.

4. The sponsorship committee follows through with their prospects a week after distributing the letters. Robin says despite this occurring during a holiday season, volunteers and staff work to ensure a commitment at this time.

Sponsorships support 90 percent of the gala funding and 100 percent of the golf invitational. The committee secures 30 sponsors on average for both events annually.

Source: Bernadette Robin, Director of Annual and Special Giving, Rutland Health Foundation, Rutland, VT. Phone (802) 747-3634. E-mail: bcrobin@rrmc.org

Content not available in this edition

Content not available in this edition

Advice for Securing Sponsorships

Robin offers the following advice when securing sponsorships:

- **Build a good committee.** "A strong volunteer committee is an organizational asset. It would be quite difficult for development professionals to structure sponsorship levels and benefits without the insight of those in the business community," says Robin.

- **Effective communication.** "Good communication with sponsors helps pave the way for future sponsorships. Make sure sponsors feel like their support was valued and that they truly helped. Robin says their website serves as a valuable tool for promoting events and sponsorships.

- **Build relationships.** "The development staff should find ways to constantly foster and build a relationship with each sponsor. Learn their names, preferences and anticipate their questions," she says.

OFFER SPONSORSHIPS AS ONE VIABLE OPTION

Corporate Sponsorship Commitment Form Helps Track Sponsorships

Special Events and Corporate Sponsorship Manager Beth Hrubesky uses this corporate sponsorship commitment form to help her keep track of several special events held both locally and regionally in support of the Girls Scouts of the Northwestern Great Lakes, Inc. (Green Bay, WI).

"It's best to take the form in and talk to sponsors in person," Hrubesky says. "If that is not possible, we mail the form with a letter that makes reference to a mutual friend. Each prospective sponsor receives a follow-up phone call by someone who believes in our mission."

The first page of the four-page form includes information about the event. For example, the Women of Courage, Confidence and Character sponsorship commitment form describes the event and includes photos of the girls the event supports. The second and third pages outline the benefits the sponsor will receive.

The fourth page of the form collects sponsors' contact information and the level of sponsorship they are choosing. It includes an area for them to indicate whether they have enclosed a check; will be mailing it, and by what date; or want to be billed.

"When a sponsor pays depends on the time of year and their budget," says Hrubesky. "We let them choose when to write out the check. I have never had a sponsor confirm their sponsorship and not pay."

The forms allow Hrubesky to track the number of sponsors for each event, and where they are in the process. Once a signed form is received, for example, a sponsor is moved from the verbal commitment category to confirmed (if accompanied by a check) and pending if not. All sponsors must have a completed and signed form on file, she says.

A thank-you letter is sent to sponsors upon receipt of each signed form.

"If they checked the box on the form that says they will pay by X date, and they have not, I may send another thank-you letter as a way to prompt them to make payment," says Hrubesky. "I never come out and ask directly for payment. I prefer to take the softer approach."

After each event, Hrubesky follows up with a handwritten note to each sponsor.

Source: Beth Hrubesky, Special Events and Corporate Sponsorship Manager, Girl Scouts of the Northwestern Great Lakes, Inc., Green Bay Service Center, Green Bay, WI. Phone (920) 469-4860, ext. 4013. E-mail: BHrubesky@gsnwgl.org

Content not available in this edition

Content not available in this edition

Content not available in this edition

OFFER SPONSORSHIPS AS ONE VIABLE OPTION

Find Companies to Sponsor Your Website

Consider asking companies to sponsor your website.

With the inception 10 years ago of the website for the Mesa Chamber of Commerce (Mesa, AZ), chamber officials sold sponsorships to offset costs and fund ongoing website improvements and as an additional revenue source for the chamber.

Pam Stapley, director of communications, says in those 10 years, the chamber has generated more than $120,000 in income, with 50 percent directed to its general fund.

Here's how the sponsorship program works:

- As many as five entities can sponsor the site at a time.

- Each sponsor pays $4,500 and must sign a two-year contract. The sponsors have first right of refusal or renewal at the end of the two-year period.

- Each sponsor is recognized with a banner ad on the home page or a logo with a link to the sponsor's page.

- Sponsors are offered category exclusivity (e.g., if there were only two beverage distribution companies in town, only one could sponsor the site at a time).

The website garners 300,000 hits a month, many from people looking to move to Mesa, Stapley says. "Our approach to businesses is that by having their logo prominently displayed on the home page, they would directly benefit from that kind of exposure."

Source: Pamela Stapley, Director Communications, Mesa Chamber of Commerce, Mesa, AZ. Phone (480) 969-1307, ext. 13. E-mail: pstapley@mesachamber.org

Get Businesses, Corporations to Sponsor Your Volunteers

Volunteers with PARACHUTE: Butler County CASA (Hamilton, OH) receive special training as court-appointed special advocates for abused and neglected children.

Officials use this volunteer-driven structure to solicit support from businesses and corporations for CASA's Sponsor a Volunteer program, says Chris Schultz, executive director. "We calculated the cost to supervise and train one volunteer to be $1,400," says Schultz. "We ask corporations if they'll support their employee who is our volunteer by donating that amount. Local companies can also sponsor a volunteer who will serve children in the part of town where the company is located."

The 30-hour classes may have two to 20 participants. Each year CASA usually has new participant sponsors. Some sponsors, such as Target and Wal-Mart, stay on for several years. A local Kiwanis club sponsored a member who became a CASA volunteer.

"One year, all 18 volunteers in a class were sponsored, while other times only one to two are sponsored," says Schultz. "We have had as few as one donor and as many as seven to sponsor an entire class."

Before the training, corporations are sent information such as number of participants and dates and times of the classes. After the training, donors receive a report with photos, information on how many volunteers completed the class and general information on type of children's cases that will be assigned to the new volunteer advocates.

Donors are also invited to a swearing-in ceremony with the judge and new CASA volunteers, and are recognized in CASA's newsletters, annual reports and in the local newspaper. CASA officials also schedule time to visit donors, sometimes with the new volunteer, to share how that CASA volunteer is helping improve children's lives.

"This strategy of soliciting donations allows a company or group to feel like they get something concrete for their donation," says Schultz. "We find that most people believe we have a mission that is important and want to help, but some may not want to take the time to join as a volunteer and go through CASA's training program. This is another way that they can get involved."

Source: Chris Schultz, Executive Director, PARACHUTE: Butler County CASA, Hamilton, OH. Phone (513) 887-3880. E-mail: PARACASA@aol.com

Advance Businesses From Sponsors to Major Donors

High-level corporate donors often start out as sponsors of events or programs. It's like landing a first-time contribution from an individual: Begin small and work your way up.

So as you increase the number of yearly sponsorships, your pool of likely major gift donors will expand as well.

The process of managing corporate donors is not unlike that of individuals. It requires implementing an ongoing set of strategies aimed at cultivating each company toward the realization of a major gift. Part of that cultivation comes

from the visibility and benefits the company receives through its sponsorships.

Keep identifying new sponsorship opportunities and approaching new companies with an invitation to sponsor whatever part of your event or program they find most appealing. As your corporate sponsor numbers grow, selectively move appropriate companies into your major gifts prospect pool.

Turning to Business for Support: How to Increase Gift Support from Businesses & Corporations

GREAT IDEAS FOR RAISING GIFTS FROM BUSINESSES

Learn to think outside the box in exploring the ways businesses might support your organization. Learn from what other nonprofits are doing successfully. Be prepared to target particular types of businesses or professions with funding ideas that will appeal to them. Following is a small sampling of ideas you can use to begin exploring new ways of generating support from businesses and corporations.

Encourage Businesses to Set Up a Matching Gift Program

Staff at the University of Louisiana at Lafayette are working hard to increase community involvement by encouraging local businesses to establish matching gift programs. Helping them do so is a sample packet explaining what matching gifts are, their tax benefits and sample matching gift forms (see sample donor form and memo, below).

"Our goal is to set up an appointment with the president of a local company and conduct a 30-minute presentation about the importance of establishing a matching gift program for employees," says Angie Eckman, assistant director of UL Lafayette's Alumni Association. "We tell them about the huge impact their participation could have on our alumni association, especially since a large number of our alumni live in our local area."

Matching gift program stipulations — such as whether it will be a one-to-one or two-to-one match — are left up to the company, says Eckman. One company that just began participating, for example, wants all contributions from employees to come directly to them, which they will then redirect, along with their match, to the university.

Connections through the university's board and friends assist in setting up appointments with local companies, she says.

"For the first company we approached, we asked a board member who was an employee there to speak to the company president about the program. The company president agreed to participate in the program. Then I and the board member employed at the company met with its human resources director to go over the packet and to see if they needed any assistance setting up the program."

Source: Angie Eckman, Assistant Director, Alumni Association, University of Louisiana at Lafayette. Lafayette, LA. Phone (337) 482-0900. E-mail: angie@louisiana.edu Website: www.louisianaalumni.org

Content not available in this edition

Content not available in this edition

Don't Overlook Generational Businesses

Don't forget that a prosperous business passed down over two or more generations may represent enormous wealth.

One measure of inherited wealth can be derived by researching the deceased's will and inventory, which are public documents and can be found at the courthouse.

Local historic books (found at the local library) can also provide family background information and their rise to prominence.

GREAT IDEAS FOR RAISING GIFTS FROM BUSINESSES

How to Chalk Up $25,000 In New Gifts From Businesses

Whether after $25,000 or $250,000, it's important to establish and stick to a fundraising plan. To secure $25,000 in new gift revenue from area businesses, consider these steps:

1. Ask a board member or business donor to establish a challenge gift that will match all new and increased gifts from businesses for the next three years.

2. Pull together a group of 25 volunteers who are committed to and contributing to your organization.

3. Ask each volunteer to help you raise $1,000 in new or increased gifts from the business community during the next 12 months. Then meet with them monthly to review progress, discuss prospect names and make new assignments.

4. Establish a club or program with benefits aimed at businesses that give at a certain level, making it hard for businesses to say "no" to volunteers' invitations to join.

Employees Help Children By Staying Home

What would you give to have an extra day to spend with family and friends over a long holiday weekend?

Staff of Pulte Homes' Raleigh division (Raleigh, NC) were hoping employees would give a lot, and they have.

Pulte Homes' employees have raised approximately $10,000 for North Carolina Children's Hospital through the company's Buy Your Way Out of Work program. Crystal Hinson Miller, director of external affairs and communications, North Carolina Children's Hospital (Chapel Hill, NC) says it's a very simple fundraiser to plan. Here's how it works:

A few weeks before the hospital's annual radiothon/telethon, division employees receive information about the program and how the money raised helps the hospital. As long as 90 percent of Pulte's employees donate at least $25 each to the challenge, all of the employees are allowed to take off the Wednesday before Thanksgiving to extend their time with family and friends.

Participation has surpassed the 90 percent threshold in each of the three years of the fundraiser. All money raised goes directly to radiothon/telethon.

In addition to the funds raised, the challenge has resulted in an ongoing partnership. Pulte Homes has adopted the hospital as its charity of choice, raising more than $23,000 for the hospital in Pulte Homes' first charity golf tournament, with plans to make it an annual event.

Source: Crystal Hinson Miller, Director of External Affairs and Communications, North Carolina Children's Hospital, Chapel Hill, NC. Phone (919) 966-5812. E-mail: hinsonmiller@med.unc.edu

Involve Architects, Engineers, Contractors

Looking for a way to reach out to architects, engineers and contractors in your area? Then this may be the ticket for you!

Canstruction® combines the competitive spirit of a design/build competition with a unique way to help feed hungry people, says Cheri Melillo, president and executive director, Canstruction (New York, NY). Competing teams, lead by architects and engineers, showcase their talents by designing giant sculptures made entirely out of cans of food.

The events are held in malls, museums, public spaces and design centers and exhibited to the public, with admission being one canned food item. At the close of the exhibitions, all of the food used in the structures is donated to local food banks for distribution to pantries, shelters, soup kitchens, elderly and day care centers, says Melillo. Last year, Canstruction competitions generated 1.5 million pounds of canned food.

Covenant House and American Institute of Architects of West Virginia (Charleston, WV) held its Canstruction event in February 2007 and raised nearly 9,500 pounds of food for the Covenant House Food Pantry. One architectural masterpiece included a mimic of the prehistoric monuments of Easter Island made of 700 cans of peas, including six-foot tall and seven-foot tall monuments.

In addition to media coverage and keeping the issues of hunger in the public eye, Melillo says a single competition can yield anywhere from 9,000 to 251,000 pounds of food. For information on having a Canstruction event, visit: www.canstruction.org.

Source: Cheri Melillo, President and Executive Director, Canstruction, New York, NY. Phone (212) 792-4666. E-mail: cmelillo@canstruction.org. Website: www.canstruction.org Amy Weintraub, Executive Director, Covenant House, Charleston, WV. Website: www.wvcovenanthouse.org

GREAT IDEAS FOR RAISING GIFTS FROM BUSINESSES

Four Ways to Increase Local Business Support

Looking for ways to increase gifts from local businesses? Try one or all of these tried-and-tested methods:

1. **Hold an honoree event.** Marie Galvin, manager of foundation relations, Rahway Hospital Foundation (Rahway, NJ), says selecting a community member who has been a good friend to your organization can have added benefits. "Holding an event that recognizes a friend to our organization while attracting new people to us is a great idea." This simultaneously promotes your organization to a new audience (honoree's friends, family and business colleagues) and a VIP reception preceding the event makes attendees feel even more special.

2. **Create giving packages that provide options.** With a variety of events and their annual fund each year, the development staff felt as though they were making repeat requests for support to the same businesses. That's why they created giving packages. Now they send support letters annually, well in advance of business budget planning. Each business chooses from all of the events and campaigns to create their own support package. The change has produced some positive results according to Galvin. "Through the giving packages, businesses were not oversolicited and we had a surprising benefit of a dramatic increase in gifts to our annual fund."

3. **Ask contributors to match their financial donations with service by joining one of your committees.** After explaining what will be expected of them, list committee member's names on your letterhead, in journals and other publications whenever possible to highlight their importance. The more invested business people are, the more likely their gifts will increase.

4. **Construct a recognition wall in your lobby.** The recognition helps encourage donors to repeat gifts and plants the giving idea in others who visit your facilities.

Source: Marie Galvin, Manager of Foundation Relations, Rahway Hospital Foundation, Rahway, NJ. Phone (732) 499-6135. E-mail: mgalvin@rwjuhr.com

Business Advisory Council Generates $50,000

Want to generate more $500 business gifts for your annual fund? Here's one idea:

1. Initiate an exclusive annual gift club for any business willing to make an annual contribution of $500 and give it a name such as The Business Advisory Council.

2. Anyone who gives at that level gets the privilege of voting how they wish to have their donations used based on recommendations from staff. Council members choose how they wish their donations to be spent.

3. To increase membership in your Business Advisory group, send an appeal directed to a targeted group of would-be donors and/ or coordinate a phonathon. In addition, host special receptions for key businesses in your community or targeted areas that includes a brief program outlining the council's goals.

If successful, your Business Advisory Council will result in $50,000 in gifts directed to a funding project (or projects) that the group has chosen collectively.

Identify Businesses That Match Hours Instead of Dollars

Corporate programs that match employee donations can be a great resource, but don't forget that some businesses prefer to match time rather than money.

"Some businesses who won't match dollars will match hours," says Annette Perry, executive director, Linn-Mar School Foundation (Marion, IA). "One man in our district raised more than $750 in one year through the time he spent as a volunteer mentor in the robotics program. By having his employer put money to those evening and weekend hours, he not only helped the students he worked with, he helped the school system as a whole."

Source: Annette Perry, Executive Director, Linn-Mar School Foundation, Marion, IA. Phone (319) 447-3065. E-mail: Aperry@linnmar.k12.ia.us

Corporate Gift Idea

Looking for a gift idea that might interest a corporation? Ask for funds to honor all of your community's top donors and volunteers for the past year. It's a way to recognize major contributors and land a corporate gift as well.

GREAT IDEAS FOR RAISING GIFTS FROM BUSINESSES

Donors Invited to Give Square Feet

Simplifying your campaign makes it easier to explain to donors and get them on board.

When faced with raising $26.6 million for a new, 66,000-square-foot Tampa Museum of Art (TMA) of Tampa, FL, officials broke it down into simple, understandable components: raising money one square foot at a time.

Donors who give $404 (cost to build a square foot) to become TMA Square Foot Society members receive a certificate, T-shirt and two-year museum membership.

This creative take on the capital campaign helps to make it affordable to a much wider range of donors as persons are invited to be a part of the legacy that will help revitalize Tampa and promote the spirit of the community through the expression of ideas.

"We talked a lot about what it costs to build a museum and the idea of cost per square foot came up," says Steve Klindt, director of development. "The amount ($404) seemed like a nice, round number and sort of an entry-level price for people to participate."

In the first two months, 83 square feet have been purchased, raising $33,000. The goal for the program is $120,000, which Klindt is confident they will make. He notes that the unique approach to supporting the project has people buying square feet as gifts for relatives and grandchildren, a boon for the museum as they offer new benefits of membership while in their temporary digs.

Source: Steve Klindt, Director of Development, Tampa Museum of Art, Tampa, FL. Phone (813) 259-1734. E-mail: steve.klindt@tampamuseum.org

Content not available in this edition

Content not available in this edition

This brochure for the TMA Square Foot Society details benefits of donating $404 — the amount needed to build one square foot of the new Tampa Museum of Art (Tampa, FL).

GREAT IDEAS FOR RAISING GIFTS FROM BUSINESSES

Consultant Boosts College's Annual Campaign

Staff with the College of St. Catherine (St. Paul, MN) have seen a 32 percent increase in total revenue since enlisting the help of an annual fund consultant five years ago, says Sarah Berger, director of the annual fund.

"The consultant (from Campbell & Company of Chicago, IL) helped us take a realistic look at our annual fund and helped us set benchmarks that made sense for our institution," Berger says. "Through the consultant's help, we changed our philosophy in order to build for the long term, rather than fixate on short-term goals."

After implementing the changes recommended by the consultant, the college experienced notable results, says Berger. In addition to an increase in total revenue:

- Gifts of $100 to $249 increased 28 percent;
- Gifts of $250 to $499 increased 31 percent; and
- The average donation climbed 27 percent to $236.

Hiring an annual fund consultant can be a wise investment for the long run of an organization, says Brian Kish, annual giving consultant, Campbell & Company.

"Often, clients worry about the higher-end prospects, which are critical, but if we don't take care of our current customers, clients and prospects, they will not be there in the future as major gift supporters," says Kish. "An annual giving program is not just about providing critical, immediate-use dollars, but building a major gift donor pipeline."

Consultants bring a new point of view to the fund process, Berger adds: "Because they aren't part of the day-to-day decision-making, they are able to critique the program and make suggestions without getting mired in the politics of the organization. Consultants can bring to the table ideas from across the country and from a variety of organizations.

And, a consultant is "a great way to fill a gap in your staff, an expert that your organization may not normally be able to afford," she says.

Adds Kish: "A consultant can obviously provide an outside and unbiased view of the program. They can look at the program objectively and identify potential hidden growth areas. A true expert can act as a partner and guide in helping a current program professional navigate the often-changing world of annual giving trends and changes."

According to Kish, an organization can expect to pay between $9,000 and $12,000 for a comprehensive audit of its annual campaign.

Sources: Sarah Berger, Director of the Annual Fund, The College of St. Catherine, St. Paul, MN.
Phone (651) 690-8840. E-mail: sberger@stkate.edu
Brian Kish, Annual Giving Consultant, Campbell & Company, Chicago, IL.
E-mail: annualgiving@campbellcompany.com

Turning to Business for Support: How to Increase Gift Support From Businesses and Corporations.
Edited by Scott C. Stevenson.
© 2010 Stevenson, Inc. Published 2010 by Stevenson, Inc.

WAYS TO RECOGNIZE AND STEWARD BUSINESS DONORS

Stewardship is both an art and a science. It's the process by which we show our unending appreciation to those who have invested in our cause. It represents the ways we show donors the impact of their giving on our organization and those we serve. Proper stewardship generally results in repeat gifts.

Key Stewardship Relations Practices

Each profession has unique customer relations principles. To excel in the fundraising profession, adhere to these practical tips for maintaining good stewardship practices:

- Acknowledge all gifts within 48 hours in as personalized a way as possible.
- Send letters to prospects confirming appointment times and the visit's purpose.
- Follow up visits with a letter summarizing key points and confirming next steps.
- Show that donors' gifts are being used as intended — progress reports, tours, etc.
- Confirm how a donor wishes to have his/her name listed in your annual report.

- Thank a donor seven times — in different ways — before asking for another gift.
- Include both spouses in the solicitation process (unless directed otherwise).
- Avoid doing end runs to get to the top decision-maker. Follow protocol.
- Be up-front about the time required for an appointment and then stick to it.
- If you are unable to answer an individual's question with confidence, assure him/her you will get the answer, and then make a point to follow up within 48 hours.
- When a donor or prospective donor takes the time to stop by your office — even without an appointment — make every effort to meet with him/her.

Donation Stewardship Outlined in Policy

Donors, rest assured. The University of Notre Dame (Notre Dame, IN) leaves no question about donation stewardship. That's because for more than 12 years, the university has used a policy that defines its rules of conduct regarding the donations it receives.

"Our obligation policy publicly shares our commitment to university donors," says Katherine Graham, senior director of development marketing, communications and stewardship. "They are more than guidelines; they are ethical statements regarding accountability."

The seven rules discuss issues such as acknowledgement, recognition, donation usage and impact reporting. The university shares its policy (shown on the right) online and in its annual stewardship report.

"We are blessed with loyal alumni, parents and friends who trust university leaders to use their gifts wisely and for the intention of the donor," Graham says. "Our Obligations of Stewardship

confirm this mutual trust in writing."

When creating such a policy, Graham says to keep the list of guidelines short, use simple language and share the policy with as many audiences as possible.

Source: Katherine Graham, Senior Director of Development Marketing, Communications and Stewardship, University of Notre Dame, Department of Development, Notre Dame, IN. Phone (574) 631-9785. E-mail: katherine.graham@nd.edu

---

The Obligations of Stewardship, University of Notre Dame (Notre Dame, IN):

As a reminder of our obligation to effectively steward contributions made to Notre Dame, the university adheres to the following guidelines:

- All gifts should be acknowledged in a timely and personal manner.
- A contribution accepted with a restricted purpose must be used for that purpose.
- If the university finds itself unable to utilize a contribution for its stated purpose, this should be communicated with the donor so that an alternative usage can be arranged.
- Whenever feasible, and especially with endowment gifts, annual impact reports should be given to the donor.
- Proper recognition should always be given to the benefactor and public recognition must be approved by the donor.
- The value of any substantial benefits resulting from contributions must be reported to each contributor.
- Contributions will be accounted for using generally accepted accounting principles, which will provide a consistent, timely and accurate reporting of all gifts into the university's official financial record.

Thank you for your enduring support of the University of Notre Dame.

WAYS TO RECOGNIZE AND STEWARD BUSINESS DONORS

Program Helps Attract Business Support and Recognize Past Donors

As a way to recognize all of the companies providing them with financial and in-kind support throughout the year, West Chester University (West Chester, PA) officials created the President's Corporate Associate (PCA) Program 10 years ago. A minimum contribution of $1,000 is required for membership in the PCA. Gifts range from $1,000 to $100,000.

"We currently have just more than 100 PCA members," says Douglas Kleintop, director of corporate relations. "Our annual average retention rate is close to 90 percent. The program gives small and large businesses alike the opportunity to get involved with the university for a minimal cost. These relationships have often developed into considerably higher gifts and a greater involvement by the company."

Each fall, the university co-hosts with a local company a breakfast recognizing the past year's members. Other benefits, says Kleintop, include:

- Complimentary tickets to the President's Gold Box during home football games, the Holiday Carol Program and Reception, business networking socials, cultural arts performances and university lectures to use internally or with corporate clients.
- The opportunity to be a corporate sponsor for special events like the President's Corporate Associates Breakfast, the Presidential Scholarship Gala, lectures, homecoming, and cultural and athletic events.
- The opportunity to network with faculty, senior administration, staff and advisers when recruiting interns and future employees, as well as explore collaborative research and various other professional development programs and partnerships.
- The chance to be a guest lecturer and/or confer with university deans to explore partnership ideas.
- The chance to participate in the Adventure by Choice team-building, indoor-outdoor program for employee and professional development.
- Priority access to facility rentals and conference services on campus.

Source: Douglas Kleintop, Director of Corporate Relations, West Chester University, West Chester, PA. Phone (610) 436-2868. E-mail: dkleintop@wcupa.edu

Promote Businesses That Support Your Work

Is your organization fortunate enough to have a few businesses supporting your cause on an ongoing or seasonal basis? If so, do all within your power to recognize and thank these important supporters.

For nearly seven years, The Women's Center & Shelter of Greater Pittsburgh (Pittsburgh, PA) has received a portion of proceeds from businesses like HipPurse (Rocky Hill, CT) and GiftBack (Centerport, NY).

HipPurse, LLC, a family-owned and operated business, donates 2 percent of the proceeds from the sales of its Hands-off collection to the shelter.

GiftBack connects individuals who wish to make a positive impact with exceptional nonprofits and causes. Ten percent of every purchase from giftback.com goes back to a charity of the purchaser's choice.

To acknowledge the generosity of these two important supporters, shelter staff devote a page on their website specifically to promoting these donor businesses.

In addition, the donor businesses are acknowledged in the shelter's newsletter, annual report and occasionally with a press release.

"Our agency benefits through financial support, and most importantly, the awareness of the issue that the business community is advancing," says DeLynda Lindsey, development associate. "Conversely, we hope that businesses benefit through increased support from our agency stakeholders. Because we have wonderful supporters, they are willing to patronize those businesses that support our cause."

Sources: Meredith Hayes, Development Associate, Special Events and Publications; DeLynda Lindsey, Development Associate; The Women's Center & Shelter of Greater Pittsburgh, Pittsburgh, PA. Phone (412) 687-8017, ext. 338 (Hayes) or ext. 316 (Lindsey). E-mail: hayesm@wcspittsburgh.org or lindseyd@wcspittsburgh.org

Don't Underestimate Power of a Donor Wall

You might not think a prominently displayed donor wall that lists major donors' names would provide much incentive for others to give. But it does.

Be sure all marketing efforts state that anyone who gives above a certain level will have his/her name listed on a handsome donor wall to be permanently displayed in a prominent location.

Consider going a step further to say that names will be categorized into three levels of giving.

Although a permanent display itself may not motivate a major gift, it can influence someone's decision to give, and it recognizes donors who make principal gifts.

WAYS TO RECOGNIZE AND STEWARD BUSINESS DONORS

Show Donors the Money (and Where It Goes)

Anything you can do to show donors how their gifts make a difference will increase donors' confidence and make them more likely to give in the future.

Colleen Townsley Brinkmann, chief marketing officer, North Texas Food Bank (Dallas, TX), says a website illustration helps show donors where their food and financial donations go.

Visitors to the organization's website (www.ntfb.org) simply click on "Donate," then "Food" to find the link to the graphic chart, "Follow Your Donation."

Shown below, the graphic illustrates how food donations benefit feeding and education programs in a 13-county area.

The page also helps educate donors and others about the work of the food pantry, which Townsley Brinkmann says is paramount: "We were having trouble getting people to understand we're not a cozy, little food pantry — we're a distribution agency. (And) by helping us you are helping tens of thousands of people."

The page averages 754 hits per month.

Source: Colleen Townsley Brinkmann, Chief Marketing Officer; Mark Armstrong, Senior Manager-Internet and New Media, North Texas Food Bank, Dallas, TX. Phone (214) 347-9594.

Website Offers Giving Tools

Visitors to the North Texas Food Bank (Dallas, TX) website find several tools to encourage gifts. For example, starting at the home page (www.ntfb.org), visitors can:

Learn how to start an actual or virtual canned food drive —
Click "Donate," "Food," and select "Conduct a Canned or Virtual Food Drive" in pop-up menu to register and receive tips for gathering food or cash gifts.

See inside the food bank — Select "About Us" and "Virtual Tour."

Share the passion — Click "Media Room" and "Video Features" for online videos explaining food bank programs and how they help combat hunger in North Texas.

This online illustration shows North Texas Food Bank donors how their gifts help others.

Content not available in this edition

WAYS TO RECOGNIZE AND STEWARD BUSINESS DONORS

Work With PR Staff to Publicize Key Gifts

Publicizing gifts made to your charity should be the rule rather than the exception.

Why? Two reasons: Because gifts beget gifts, and such publicity can provide very deserving recognition to the donor. While it is true that some donors prefer low profiles and some even insist on anonymity, most donors — whether they admit it or not — find gratification in being recognized for their generosity.

Define minimum standards of what you deem noteworthy gifts — based on criteria such as gift size, gift type, donor type, etc. — and develop a system for publicizing those gifts and the persons who made them.

Begin the publicity process by seeking formal permission of the donor to publicize the gift. Explain that maximizing publicity of gifts to your institution helps encourage other members of the public to consider possible gifts of their own. Approaching the donor in this way helps to diminish any awkwardness the individual may feel about perceived self-indulgence.

Develop a publicity approval form such as the one shown here as part of a system that secures donors' approval for news release purposes to both protect your organization and encourage your publicity department to develop stories or news releases for the media.

PUBLICITY APPROVAL FORM

Name(s) of Donor(s) _____

Daytime Phone _____

Approximate Date of Gift _____

Staff Contact _____

Amount of Gift _____

Type of Gift _____

Intended Use of Gift _____

Information About the Donor(s) _____

_____

Donor Quotes _____

_____

CEO Quotes _____

_____

Quotes from Others _____

_____

❑ The donor has given publicity approval.

Staff Person/Title _____

Authorizing Approval _____

❑ *Article requires staff review before release.*

❑ *Article requires no staff review before release.*

Acknowledge Matching Gifts With a Postcard

About a year ago, staff with Augustana College (Rock Island, IL) began acknowledging receipt of matching gifts with a simple postcard.

"Previously, our institution acknowledged to a donor that a match was submitted, but did not communicate that the match money had arrived, except to include the value in gift club recognition for the fiscal year," says Anne E. Bergren, director of donor relations and stewardship.

She says they chose a postcard rather than a traditional letter and envelope for two reasons: First, the lower postage cost, and second, the ease of communicating the message. "A postcard doesn't need to be opened for the message to be seen, thereby eliminating the 'toss the envelope without opening it' scenario."

The postcard simply informs donors that Augustana officials have received their matching gift and thanks them for making the gift. Bergren signs each card.

She notes that donors have commented that they appreciate knowing the college has obtained the match.

Source: Anne E. Bergren, Director of Donor Relations and Stewardship, Augustana College, Rock Island, IL. Phone (309) 794-7228. E-mail: Anne-Bergren@augustana.edu

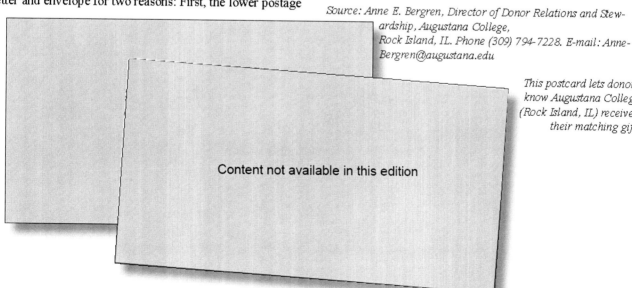

This postcard lets donors know Augustana College (Rock Island, IL) received their matching gift.

Content not available in this edition

WAYS TO RECOGNIZE AND STEWARD BUSINESS DONORS

Encourage Employees to Thank Their Employers

There's nothing forcing employers to establish or maintain matching gifts programs for their employees. That's why nonprofits that benefit from those gifts should take steps to show appreciation.

Help donors who work for matching gift companies say thanks on your behalf by providing them with a sample letter they can use to craft their own notes or letters of appreciation. Grateful notes from employees will carry even more weight than a letter from your nonprofit.

Develop one or more letters, such as the generic example shown here, and share them with your contributors who work for matching gift companies. Encourage them to use your example as a guide in thanking their employers for making a matching gift possible.

Dear [Name of Employer]:

I simply want to join [name of your nonprofit] in thanking you for recently making a matching gift on my behalf. Your matching gift program helps motivate me to give as generously as possible knowing you will match my gift dollar for dollar.

I recognize that it's a company choice to have this matching gift program and I want to tell you how much it means to me and to [name of nonprofit] and those who benefit from its services.

I hope you continue to keep this program in place for many years to come.

Sincerely,

[Your name]

Unique Illustration Recognizes Top Donors

You would like to recognize a high-end donor with a feature article and photo in an upcoming publication but are tired of the traditional approach? Consider putting a new twist on the old with an illustration rather than a photo.

Officials with the Fashion Institute of Technology (New York, NY) developed signage to honor a couple who had donated $10 million to the institution.

Carol Leven, assistant vice president for communications, says the institution was naming one of the schools after the donors. To commemorate the occasion a cast aluminum sign would be placed in one of the buildings. "We were including an illustration on the sign and we needed a new and creative technique. Our design firm came up with the solution to have a pointillist portrait illustration of the couple etched on the sign."

Leven says the illustration was also a way to step away from the traditional headshots. "This is a very different

medium. It can humanize people, make people feel special and capture something about them and their personality in a way that a photograph cannot."

Wall Street Journal illustrator Nolie Novacks was chosen to work on the illustration for the sign. Leven says because Novacks was able to work from a photograph, they chose a photo of the couple taken the year before. The project took three weeks to complete.

Illustrations can range from $300 to $2,000, depending on the extent of the work, and Leven says a variety of styles are available from sketches to paintings.

The college expanded this concept to several areas including their redesigned alumni magazine.

Source: Carol Leven, Assistant Vice President for Communications, Fashion Institute of Technology, Office of College Relations, New York, NY. Phone (212) 217-7642. E-mail: carol_leven@fitnyc.edu

Content not available in this edition

9 781118 692189